WEAPONS OF THE FALKLANDS CONFLICT

To my wife Anne,
who helped in so many ways

WEAPONS
of the
FALKLANDS CONFLICT

Bryan Perrett

BLANDFORD PRESS
Poole   Dorset

First published in the U.K. 1982 by Blandford Press,
Link House, West Street, Poole, Dorset, BH15 1LL

Copyright © 1982 Bryan Perrett
Reprinted in 1983 (twice)
Reprinted in paperback 1984

Distributed in the United States by
Sterling Publishing Co., Inc.,
2 Park Avenue, New York, N.Y. 10016

British Library Cataloguing in Publication Data

Perrett, Bryan
  Weapons of the Falklands conflict.
  1. Falkland Islands War, 1982
  2. Great Britain—Armed forces—Equipment
  3. Argentina—Armed forces—Equipment
  I. Title
  623'.0941   UC525.G7

ISBN 0 7137 1315 1 (hardback)
ISBN 0 7137 1450 6 (paperback)

Typeset by August Filmsetting, Warrington, Cheshire.
Printed in Great Britain by Biddles of Guildford Ltd, Surrey.

Contents

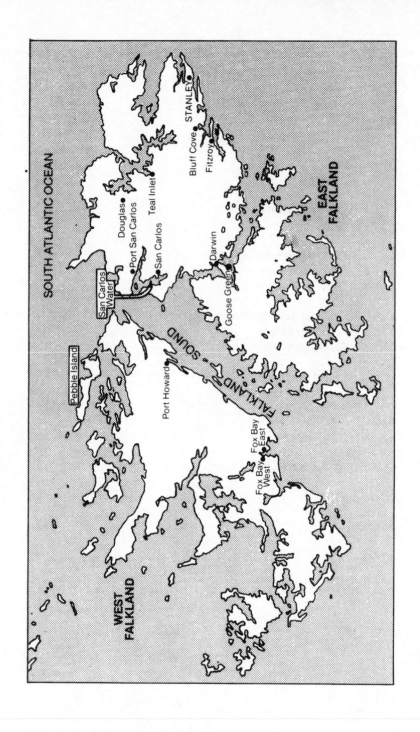

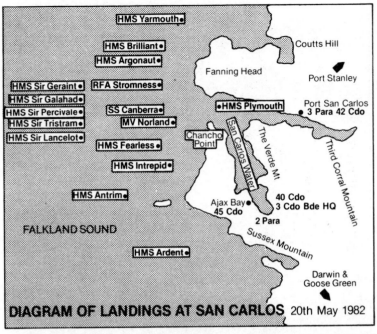

DIAGRAM OF LANDINGS AT SAN CARLOS 20th May 1982

Labels on diagram:
- HMS Yarmouth
- HMS Brilliant
- HMS Argonaut
- HMS Sir Geraint
- RFA Stromness
- HMS Sir Galahad
- HMS Sir Percivale
- HMS Sir Tristram
- HMS Sir Lancelot
- SS Canberra
- MV Norland
- HMS Fearless
- HMS Intrepid
- HMS Antrim
- FALKLAND SOUND
- HMS Ardent
- Coutts Hill
- Fanning Head
- Port Stanley
- HMS Plymouth
- Port San Carlos 3 Para 42 Cdo
- Chancho Point
- San Carlos Water
- The Verde Mt
- Third Corral Mountain
- Ajax Bay 45 Cdo
- 40 Cdo 3 Cdo Bde HQ
- 2 Para
- Sussex Mountain
- Darwin & Goose Green

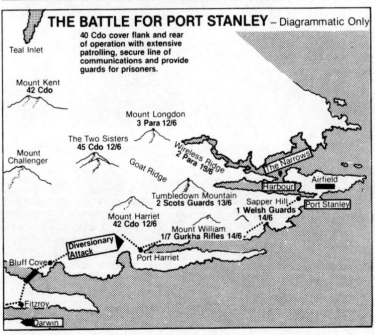

THE BATTLE FOR PORT STANLEY – Diagrammatic Only

40 Cdo cover flank and rear of operation with extensive patrolling, secure line of communications and provide guards for prisoners.

Labels on diagram:
- Teal Inlet
- Mount Kent 42 Cdo
- Mount Longdon 3 Para 12/6
- The Two Sisters 45 Cdo 12/6
- Mount Challenger
- Goat Ridge
- Wireless Ridge 2 Para 13/6
- The Narrows
- Airfield
- Harbour
- Tumbledown Mountain 2 Scots Guards 13/6
- Sapper Hill 1 Welsh Guards 14/6
- Port Stanley
- Mount Harriet 42 Cdo 12/6
- Mount William 1/7 Gurkha Rifles 14/6
- Diversionary Attack
- Bluff Cove
- Port Harriet
- Fitzroy
- Darwin

Introduction

In the early hours of 2 April 1982 Argentine armed forces landed at Port Stanley in the Falkland Islands and the following day at Grytviken on South Georgia. Both landings succeeded against the token Royal Marine garrisons and Argentina quickly took control of the islands. Only 72 hours after the invasion the first elements of the British Task Force, led by the carriers *Hermes* and *Invincible*, were clearing Portsmouth Harbour and steaming south.

The gathering of the Task Force and its fitting out was one of the greatest achievements of the Falklands war, and was staggeringly successful by any standards. For following in the wake of *Hermes*, *Invincible* and their escorts would come warships from every base in the United Kingdom and the Mediterranean, Royal Fleet Auxiliary Service vessels, and requisitioned merchant vessels of all kinds from the stately 67,000-ton *Queen Elizabeth 2* to the little tugs *Yorkshireman* and *Irishman*, displacing only 690 tons. Altogether, more than 100 ships and some 30,000 men would be directly involved in the venture.

The logistic computations were formidable. Men, machines, weapons, ammunition, fuel, food and spares had to arrive at the dockside at exactly the right time and in the right order for correct operational loading. For each ship the loading schedules ran into tens of thousands of items. The list was endless: Harriers, helicopters, tanks, guns, lorries, Land Rovers, armoured recovery vehicles, combat engineer tractors, field engineering stores, earth movers, communications and electronic warfare equipment, missiles of all types, bombs, ground attack rockets, anti-tank rounds, grenades, thousands of shells, millions of rounds of small arms ammunition, medical supplies of every type, tents, clothing, boots, ration packs and, by no means unimportant, thousands of gallons of beer.

It all reflected years of continuous work within the

Ministry of Defence, for if the Warsaw Pact ever did choose war as an extension of its policies the speedy reinforcement of the Rhine Army held absolute priority. Consequently, the location of every item and its means of delivery was known long before hostilities in the South Atlantic commenced.

The 3rd Commando Brigade (40, 42 and 45 Commandos), reinforced by the 2nd and 3rd Battalions, The Parachute Regiment, were detailed for the first wave of the assault, and left aboard the liner *Canberra*. The 5th Infantry Brigade (2nd Battalion, The Scots Guards, 1st Battalion, The Welsh Guards and 1st/7th Gurkha Rifles) were to follow aboard the *Queen Elizabeth 2*. There was also a strong contingent from the 22nd Special Air Service Regiment and its Royal Marine equivalent, both with an international reputation for clandestine operations ruthlessly and efficiently executed; there were, too, units from every walk of service life, including the Blues and Royals, who would man the light tanks which had been embarked, the Royal Artillery, the Army Air Corps, the Royal Engineers, the Royal Electrical and Mechanical Engineers, the Royal Corps of Signals, the Royal Corps of Transport, the Royal Army Ordnance Corps, the Royal Army Medical Corps and the service nursing organisations, the Royal Corps of Military Police, the Army Catering Corps and specialist Royal Air Force personnel.

Approximately halfway between the United Kingdom and the Falklands lies Ascension Island which remains a British possession. Here the Task Force was sorted into its various fighting and support elements, the skies above busy with RAF Hercules transports and VC 10s, hired Boeing 707s and Belfasts, flying in yet more troops and supplies; there were American transport aircraft, too, for the United States was providing Britain with material aid. Here also the Task Force commander, Rear-Admiral John Woodward, a former submariner and Director of Naval Planning at the Ministry of Defence, came aboard and hoisted his flag in HMS *Hermes*.

The problems facing Admiral Woodward were immense and there were no easy answers to any of them. First, he would have to wrest control of the sea from a fleet which, although admittedly smaller than his own, possessed equally powerful weapons and which, if handled with aggression and skill, had the capacity to inflict very serious loss. Secondly, and of paramount importance, he would somehow have to attain air superiority in circumstances in which his first wave of 20 Harriers was outnumbered by ten to one. Thirdly, he would have to execute an amphibious landing, which might or might not be opposed. Fourthly, he would have to maintain support for the ground troops until the invaders had been ejected.

On 7 April the British government declared a 200-mile (322 km) exclusion zone around the Falklands, dropping some heavy hints that nuclear-powered hunter-killer submarines were in a position to enforce the blockade. The result was that seaborne supply and reinforcement of the junta's garrison, now estimated at 10,000 fully equipped men, was reduced to a trickle, although an air bridge between mainland bases and Port Stanley airfield remained in operation.

The Task Force continued to sail south and on 25 April the destroyer *Antrim*, the frigate *Plymouth* and the ice patrol ship *Endurance*, which had never left her station, effected the recapture of South Georgia. In the process the Argentine submarine *Santa Fe* was crippled by fire from the ships' helicopters and hastily abandoned by her crew. Argentine casualties were light and for the British the victory was bloodless.

The battle proper for the Falklands began on 1 May with an attempt to destroy the islands' end of the Argentine air bridge. A Vulcan bomber, flying from Ascension Island and refuelled in flight by a Victor tanker, raided Port Stanley airfield, which was later attacked by Harriers and subjected to the first of many bombardments by units of the fleet. Elsewhere, the Harriers attacked aircraft parked on the grass airstrip at Goose Green and in the first aerial combats proved that they were more than a match for the Argentine Mirages, two of which were shot down as well as one, and probably two, Canberra bombers.

On 2 May the cruiser *General Belgrano*, the second largest warship Argentina possessed, was torpedoed twice by a British hunter-killer submarine and sank with heavy loss of life. During the next 36 hours Task Force helicopters engaged four armed patrol ships with their Sea Skua missiles, sinking two, running a third aground and severely damaging the fourth. Following these losses the Argentine Navy all but retired from the conflict.

Perversely, world opinion now took the view that the British were handing out *too* much of a beating to their opponents. That impression was sharply corrected on 4 May when HMS *Sheffield* was struck by an air-launched Exocet missile. Twenty of her crew died and fires gutted the ship, effectively destroying her. On the same day a Harrier was shot down by ground fire and two days later two further Harriers were lost in a mid-air collision. The war was far from being one-sided. The naval and air exclusion zone was extended to within 12 miles (19 km) of the Argentine mainland.

Air and sea attacks continued on objectives around the islands. On 9 May an enemy Puma troop-carrying helicopter was shot down near Port Stanley while at sea two Harriers engaged and strafed a fishing vessel that was behaving suspiciously. The crew surrendered and the vessel, named *Narwal*, was boarded from a helicopter and found to be a spy ship with two naval officers on board and written instructions to report on Task Force dispositions.

On 11 May the frigate *Alacrity* entered Falkland Sound during the hours of darkness. Firing starshells, she flushed out a freighter which tried to run from her. *Alacrity* opened up with her 4.5-inch gun and after only a few rounds had been fired the freighter disintegrated in a tremendous explosion which suggested that she was an ammunition carrier. Later the Argentines announced that one of their merchant ships, the *Islas de Los Estados*, had been reported missing.

The following day the Argentine air force, Fuerza Aerea Argentina (FAA), came out hoping to equal the score. Two flights each of two Skyhawks pounced on an isolated picket consisting of two destroyers. The encounter predicted accurately the nature of the fighting to come. Two Skyhawks were blown apart, one flew into the sea trying to avoid a missile, and the sole survivor made off. One destroyer sustained minor damage when a bomb passed straight through her hull from side to side, incredibly without exploding.

During the night of 15/16 May 48 men of the SAS carried out a successful raid on an enemy airstrip situated on Pebble

Island, off the north coast of West Falkland. Under cover of naval gunfire, meticulously controlled by a Royal Artillery observer who had accompanied the raiders, casualties were inflicted and eleven aircraft, including six ground attack Pucaras, were destroyed without loss.

Bombardment of Argentine installations, particularly around Port Stanley and its airfield, had now become a nightly occurrence. SAS and SBS teams were operating ashore and their reports indicated that the Argentine commander, General Mario Menendez, had developed a siege mentality. By far the greatest number of his troops were manning positions close to Port Stanley, but he also had moderately sized garrisons at Goose Green on the isthmus connecting the northern and southern halves of East Falkland, and at Fox Bay on West Falkland. Elsewhere, there were only small detachments. Further, the Argentines' morale was said to have been adversely affected by the policy of slow strangulation, by the climate, and by the results of the fighting thus far.

It was exactly the news Admiral Woodward had been waiting for, as he had no wish to keep his troops afloat any longer than necessary in the worsening winter seas. By coincidence, the last diplomatic initiative to resolve the issue peacefully had just failed conclusively. During the night of 20/21 May the assault wave and its escorts slipped into Falkland Sound and thence into the sheltered anchorage of San Carlos Water. Troops, tanks and Rapier air-defence missiles began streaming ashore by landing craft and helicopter. To all intents and purposes the landing was virtually unopposed. The 200-strong Argentine garrison on Fanning Head opened fire briefly but were promptly silenced by naval gunfire and chased off in the direction of Port Stanley; they had by no means had all the fight knocked out of them, however, for during their long walk they managed to shoot down two Army Air Corps Gazelle scout helicopters. This apart, what many had feared would be a bloodbath had been achieved without one single casualty from enemy action, although at sea a helicopter accident claimed the lives of 22 men, the majority of them members of the SAS.

Only the FAA showed any positive reaction. Throughout

21 May it threw every aircraft it could muster against the ships in San Carlos Water and Falkland Sound. Several of its bombs failed to explode but the frigate *Ardent* was hit repeatedly by rockets, caught fire and went down fighting. But the combined air defence of Harriers, missiles and machine gun fire held good and by sunset 17 Argentine aircraft – Mirages, Skyhawks, Pucaras and helicopters – had been shot down, about 50 per cent of those involved.

Saturday 22 May can be regarded as the day on which Argentina lost the war, for while the FAA stayed at home to reorganise, the beachhead defences were consolidated and the Royal Engineers began building landing pads for the RAF Harriers being carried aboard the *Atlantic Conveyor*.

The following day the FAA returned to the fray, the skill and bravery of its pilots earning the sincere admiration of their enemies. Again several bombs failed to explode and it was clear that either something was wrong with their fusing mechanism, or that the bombing technique itself was faulty. One bomb, however, lodged deep inside the frigate *Antelope* and detonated while attempts were being made to defuse it. Once more fire raged through a warship despite the valiant efforts of her crew to control the spreading inferno, and eventually she had to be abandoned; *Antelope* was to explode in a horrendous fireball during the night. When the day ended a further 11 Argentine aircraft had been destroyed.

The FAA came back again on 24 May and this time it made the beachhead its primary target. A few casualties were caused and an ammunition dump set on fire, but eight Argentine aircraft were lost. Argentina's National Day is 25 May and nothing was more certain than that the FAA would make a serious attempt to destroy a prestigious target. During the afternoon four Skyhawks attacked the destroyers *Broadsword* and *Coventry* while they were on radar picket north of the Falklands. All four were blown out of the sky, as was a reconnaissance aircraft which ventured too close. A little later, however, four more Skyhawks came in low across Pebble Island and pressed home their attack. *Coventry* was hit repeatedly and eventually capsized, 21 of her crew being killed. The remainder were taken off by *Broadsword*, herself slightly damaged.

Argentine Super Etendards with their air-launched Exocet missiles were also out that afternoon. Two Exocets at least are known to have been fired; one did not find a target, but the second struck the *Atlantic Conveyor*, blowing a huge hole in her side and starting the fires which were to lead to her being abandoned and eventually lost. For the Task Force this was very serious indeed for although her priceless Harriers had been flown off, her cargo included all but one of the available Chinook heavy-lift helicopters. Their absence was to have a profound effect.

For the moment the FAA seemed to have shot its bolt. Consolidation of the beachhead continued throughout 26 May and next day the 3rd Commando Brigade began moving on Port Stanley by way of Douglas and Teal Inlet, the 2nd Battalion, The Parachute Regiment being detached for the elimination of the enemy garrison at Goose Green.

On Friday 28 May '2 Para' fought an enemy who out-numbered them by three to one and who had the benefit of fighting from prepared positions. Goose Green was captured after some of the most ferocious fighting of the campaign, the cost to the 2nd Battalion being its commanding officer and 17 of its officers and men killed, and twice that number wounded; the Argentines were decimated, losing 250 dead, a similar number wounded and 1,400 men taken prisoner. During the battle cloud cover prevented the Harriers giving direct support, but six Argentine Pucaras joined in, shooting down a Gazelle helicopter before four of them were despatched by Blowpipe missiles.

Elsewhere on 28 May British troops reached Douglas and Teal Inlet, while on 2 June the 1,500-foot (463 m) Mount Kent, overlooking the enemy's positions all the way to Port Stanley, was taken after a brief skirmish. Helicopters at once brought up the Royal Artillery's 105 mm light guns, and these began adding their battering to that of the Harriers and the warships.

There was now a brief deceleration in the tempo of major operations. The Port Stanley garrison was boxed in but the British land forces commander, Major-General Jeremy Moore, needed more troops before he could launch a successful assault. The 5th Infantry Brigade was, in fact, already entering the operational zone, having transferred from the *Queen Elizabeth 2* to landing ships off South Georgia. The Gurkhas came ashore and began moving along the high ground which flanked the route from Darwin to Port Stanley.

It was discovered that the civilian telephone system was still working. The 5th Infantry Brigade's commander, Brigadier Tony Wilson, put through a call to a farm manager named Reg Binney, who lived at Fitzroy. Binney told him that the small Argentine garrison had left and was believed to have pulled back into the Port Stanley perimeter. Wilson collected sufficient helicopters to lift enough men forward to occupy the abandoned position, while the Scots and Welsh Guards sailed round the island from San Carlos Water to Bluff Cove. They would travel aboard the logistic landing ships *Sir Galahad* and *Sir Tristram*.

When the two ships entered Bluff Cove on 8 June their presence was immediately detected by sophisticated West-inghouse radar sets which the Argentines had set up on the summits of Sapper Hill and the Two Sisters. Their purpose was obvious and the FAA returned to the attack. Its pilots had now learned what had been wrong with their bombing technique, which they adjusted accordingly. *Sir Tristram* was severely damaged and *Sir Galahad* turned into a raging pyre in which 50 men died. The frigate *Plymouth* was also damaged in Falkland Sound on what was unquestionably the worst day of the war for Great Britain. In fact 8 June represented the FAA's swan song, for it had sustained the loss of another 11 aircraft and played little further part in the campaign.

There was to be one further British naval casualty. On 12 June HMS *Glamorgan*, bombarding targets in the Port Stanley area, was hit by a shore-launched Exocet missile. Nine of her men died but *Glamorgan* survived, proving that Exocet was not necessarily a killer.

Meanwhile, the land battle continued. Using night-fighting techniques developed for their NATO role, British troops forced the enemy off one feature after another – Mount Longdon, Tumbledown Mountain, the Two Sisters, Sapper Hill, Wireless Ridge. By the morning of 14 June it was already apparent that Argentine discipline was beginning to break down, and suddenly the enemy's resolve cracked. Men began leaving the line, walking aimlessly towards Port Stanley, a broken army. A meeting between the two commanders was arranged and General Menendez signed a surrender document, deleting only the word 'unconditional' as a salve to his pride. It mattered not one jot, for the surrender terms included those troops on West Falkland as well, and the war was over.

On the islands, General Moore suddenly found himself responsible for 8,000 prisoners. For humanitarian reasons alone it was necessary that they be shipped back to Argentina as quickly as possible, and to this their own government agreed. The *Canberra* played a major part in this repatriation.

It had been a short, sharp and very instructive battle in which only the human factors remained constant. The effects of the weapons used and the lessons arising therefrom would be studied in minute detail from Washington to Moscow, and it was already clear that a great many of the textbooks were in need of revision.

I

The naval battle

I. THE HARDWARE

Ships of the Royal Navy

'SWIFTSURE' CLASS FLEET SUBMARINES

Submarines in class: HMS *Swiftsure*
HMS *Sovereign*
HMS *Superb*
HMS *Sceptre*
HMS *Spartan*
HMS *Splendid*

Displacement: 4,200 tons standard
4,500 tons submerged
Propulsion: nuclear reactor/geared steam turbine
diesel auxiliary
Speed: 30 knots submerged
Complement: 12 officers
85 ratings
Armament: 5 × 21-inch (533 mm) torpedo tubes firing either conventional or Tigerfish guided torpedoes. Individual torpedo reloading time, 15 seconds

Two members of this class of long endurance hunter-killer submarines, *Spartan* and *Splendid*, are known to have served in the war zone; HMS *Superb* was incorrectly reported to be in the war zone during the early days of the conflict.

'VALIANT' CLASS FLEET SUBMARINES

Submarines in class: HMS *Valiant*
                        HMS *Warspite*
                        HMS *Churchill*
                        HMS *Conqueror*
                        HMS *Courageous*

Displacement: 4,400 tons standard
                     4,900 tons submerged
Propulsion: nuclear reactor/geared steam turbine
Speed: 28 knots submerged
Complement: 13 officers
                     90 ratings
Armament: 6 × 21-inch (533 mm) torpedo tubes firing
                     either conventional or Tigerfish guided tor-
                     pedoes. Individual torpedo reloading time,
                     15 seconds

In 1967 *Valiant* completed the 12,000-mile (19,300 km) voyage from Singapore to the United Kingdom in 28 days, a British record for a submerged passage. *Conqueror* is believed to have been the only representative of her class to serve in the war zone.

ANTI-SUBMARINE WARFARE/COMMANDO CARRIER

HMS *Hermes*

Displacement: 28,700 tons
Speed: 28 knots
Complement: 143 officers
                     1,207 ratings
                     accommodation for 1 Royal Marine
                     Commando
Aircraft: 5 Sea Harriers
               9 Sea King helicopters

Missiles: 2 quad Seacat launchers
Armour: 0.75 inches (19 mm) on flight deck, up to 2 inches
            (51 mm) above magazines and machinery spaces

Hermes was built by Vickers' Barrow-in-Furness yard and was commissioned as a conventional carrier in November 1959. Between 1971 and 1973 she was converted to the commando role, her steam catapults and arrester gear being removed. In 1977 she underwent a further refit as an anti-submarine warfare carrier, although her commando role was retained.

LIGHT AIRCRAFT CARRIER

HMS *Invincible*

Displacement: 19,500 tons
Speed: 28 knots
Complement: 131 officers
              869 ratings
Aircraft: 5 Sea Harriers
          10 Sea King Helicopters
Missiles: 1 twin Sea Dart launcher

Invincible, the first of her class, was built by Vickers at Barrow-in-Furness and was commissioned on 11 June 1980. She is designed specifically for the joint operation of Sea Harriers and helicopters and is equipped with command facilities for maritime air operations.

TYPE 82 LIGHT CRUISER

HMS *Bristol*

Displacement: 7,100 tons
Speed: 28 knots

Complement: 29 officers
                 378 ratings
Aircraft: none – landing platforms for Wasp helicopter
ASW weapons: 1 Ikara launcher
Missiles: 1 twin Sea Dart launcher
Guns: 1 × 4.5 inch (114 mm)
             2 × 20 mm

Bristol was built by Swan Hunter Ltd. and commissioned in March 1973. The Type 82 light cruisers were intended as escorts for the Royal Navy's fixed-wing aircraft carriers, but when the latter were dispensed with the construction programme was discontinued after *Bristol* had been completed.

'COUNTY' CLASS DESTROYERS

Present with Task Force: HMS *Antrim*
                               HMS *Glamorgan*

Displacement: 6,200 tons
Speed: 30 knots
Complement: 33 officers
                 438 ratings
Aircraft: 1 Wessex helicopter
Missiles: 4 Exocet launchers
             1 twin Seaslug launcher
             2 quad Seacat launchers
Guns: 2 × 4.5 inch (114 mm)
             2 × 20 mm

TYPE 22 DESTROYERS

Present with Task Force: HMS *Broadsword*
                               HMS *Brilliant*

Joined by: HMS *Battleaxe*

Displacement: 4,000 tons
Speed: 30 knots
Complement: 18 officers
                        205 ratings
Aircraft: 2 Lynx helicopters
Missiles: 4 Exocet launchers
                        2 × 6-barrelled Seawolf launchers
ASW weapons: 6 tubes for Mk 46 torpedoes
                        helicopter-launched torpedoes
Guns: 2 × 40 mm

The Type 22 destroyers are primarily designed for anti-submarine warfare and are equiped as helicopter-control ships.

TYPE 42 DESTROYERS

Present with Task Force: HMS *Sheffield*
                                          HMS *Glasgow*
                                          HMS *Exeter*
                                          HMS *Coventry*

Joined by: HMS *Southampton*
                                          HMS *Cardiff*

Displacement: 4,100–4,700 tons
Speed: 29 knots
Complement: 21 officers
                        249 ratings
Aircraft: 1 Lynx helicopter
Missiles: 1 twin Sea Dart launcher
ASW weapons   6 torpedo tubes
                        helicopter-launched torpedoes
Guns: 1 × 4.5 inch (114 mm)
            2 × 20 mm Oerlikon

'LEANDER' CLASS FRIGATES

IKARA GROUP
Joined Task Force: HMS *Aurora*
                        HMS *Dido*
                        HMS *Euryalus*

Displacement: 2,860 tons
Speed: 28 knots
Complement: 19 officers
                238 ratings
Aircraft: 1 Wasp or Lynx helicopter
Missiles: 2 quad Seacat launchers
ASW weapons: 1 Ikara launcher
                1 Limbo mortar
Guns: 2 × 40 mm Bofors

EXOCET GROUP
Joined Task Force: HMS *Argonaut*
                        HMS *Minerva*

Displacement: 3,200 tons
Speed: 28 knots
Complement: 20 officers
                203 ratings
Aircraft: 1 Wasp or Lynx helicopter
Missiles: 4 Exocet launchers
                3 quad Seacat launchers
ASW weapons: 6 torpedo tubes
Guns: 2 × 40 mm Bofors

BROAD-BEAMED GROUP
Joined Task Force: HMS *Andromeda*
                        HMS *Ariadne*

Displacement: 2,962 tons
Speed: 28 knots
Complement: 19 officers
                241 ratings
Aircraft: 1 Wasp or Lynx helicopter

Missiles: 1 quad Seacat launcher
             (*Andromeda* converted: 4 Exocet, 1 Seawolf)
ASW weapons: 1 Limbo mortar
                (*Andromeda* converted: torpedo tubes)
Guns: 2 × 4.5 inch (114 mm)
         2 × 20 mm
         (*Andromeda* converted: 2 × 20 mm)

TYPE 21 FRIGATES

Present with Task Force: HMS *Ardent*
                           HMS *Alacrity*
                           HMS *Antelope*
                           HMS *Arrow*

Joined by: HMS *Active*
                           HMS *Avenger*
                           HMS *Ambuscade*

Displacement: 3,250 tons
Speed: 30 knots
Complement: 13 officers
               162 ratings
Aircraft: 1 Lynx or Wasp helicopter
Missiles: 4 Exocet launchers
             1 quad Seacat launcher
ASW weapons: 6 torpedo tubes
                helicopter-launched torpedoes
Guns: 1 × 4.5 inch (114 mm)
         2 × 20 mm Oerlikon

MODIFIED TYPE 12 FRIGATES

Present with Task Force: HMS *Yarmouth*
                           HMS *Plymouth*

Joined by: HMS *Berwick*
                              HMS *Falmouth*
                              HMS *Rhyl*

Displacement: 2,800 tons
Speed: 30 knots
Complement: 15 officers
                      220 ratings
Aircraft: 1 Wasp helicopter
Missiles: 1 quad Seacat launcher
ASW weapons: 1 Limbo mortar
Guns: 2 × 4.5 inch (114 mm)

TYPE 81 'TRIBAL' CLASS FRIGATE

Joined Task Force: HMS *Tartar*

Displacement: 2,700 tons
Speed: 25 knots
Complement: 13 officers
                      240 ratings
Aircraft: 1 Wasp helicopter
Missiles: 2 quad Seacat launchers
ASW weapons: 1 Limbo mortar
Guns: 2 × 4.5 inch (114 mm)
          2 × 20 mm

ASSAULT SHIPS

Present with Task Force: HMS *Fearless*
                                  HMS *Intrepid*

Displacement: 12,120 tons loaded
                    16,950 tons dock flooded
Speed: 21 knots

Complement: 580, including 400 troops in normal accommodation
700 troops for short periods
Aircraft: space for 5 Wessex helicopters on flight deck
Missiles: 4 quad Seacat launchers
Guns: 2 × 40 mm Bofors
Landing craft: 4 LCM(9) inboard in dock, being floated out through open stern, once ship has been lowered in water by controlled flooding, and carrying 2 main battle tanks or 100 tons weight.
4 LCVP slung from davits, each carrying 2 Land Rovers or 35 men.

Fearless and *Intrepid* are both fitted out as naval assault group/brigade headquarters with fully equiped control rooms. A specimen load might consist of 15 main battle tanks, 7 × 3-ton trucks and 20 Land Rovers.

LOGISTIC LANDING SHIPS

Present with Task Force: HMS *Sir Lancelot*
HMS *Sir Geraint*
HMS *Sir Galahad*
HMS *Sir Tristram*
HMS *Sir Bedivere*
HMS *Sir Percivale*

Displacement: 5,674 tons
Speed: 17 knots
Complement: 18 officers
50 ratings
340 troops in normal accommodation
534 troops hard lying
Aircraft: none, but helicopters can be operated from well deck and aft platform
Guns: 2 × 40 mm Bofors

Cranes: 1 × 20-ton
          2 × 4.5-ton
Capacity: 16 main battle tanks or 34 mixed vehicles
          120 tons of petrol, oil and lubricants
          30 tons of ammunition
          alternatively, 11 helicopters can be stowed on tank deck and 9 on vehicle deck

These ships are equipped for either bow or stern loading, offer drive-through facilities and have inter-deck vehicle ramps. Although Royal Navy vessels, they are manned by Royal Fleet Auxiliary Service personnel, many of whom are recruited in Hong Kong.

SURVEY SHIPS

Present with Task Force: HMS *Herald*
                                HMS *Hecla*
                                HMS *Hydra*

Displacement: 2,733/2,945 tons
Speed: 14 knots
Complement: 128 officers and men
Aircraft: 1 Wasp helicopter
Armament: none

Converted for use as hospital ships.

ICE PATROL SHIP

HMS *Endurance* (ex-*Anita Dan*)

Displacement: 3,600 tons
Speed: 14.5 knots

Complement: 13 officers
                 106 ratings, including small Royal
                 Marine detachment
Aircraft carried: 2 Wasp helicopters
Missiles: none
Guns: 2 × 20 mm

HMS *Endurance* is stationed off the Falkland Islands and the dependencies. Its hull is painted red for easy identification by landing parties working on the ice.

Royal Fleet Auxiliary Service Vessels Accompanying the Task Force

RFA *Olmeda*, large fleet tanker
Displacement: 10,890/36,000 tons
Speed: 19 knots
Complement: 87
Aircraft: 4 Sea King helicopters

RFA *Tidespring*, large fleet tanker
Displacement: 8,531/27,400 tons
Speed: 18.3 knots
Complement: 110
Aircraft: 4 Sea King helicopters

RFA *Appleleaf* and RFA *Brambleleaf*, support tankers
Displacement: 40,200 full load
Speed: 15.5 knots

RFA *Pearleaf*, support tanker
Displacement: 25,790 tons full load
Speed: 16 knots
Complement: 55

RFA *Resource*, fleet replenishment ship AEFS (ammunition, explosives, food and stores)

Displacement: 22,890 tons full load
Speed: 21 knots
Complement: 119   RFA   personnel   plus   Royal   Navy
                detachment
Aircraft: 4 Sea King helicopters
Guns: 2 × 40 mm Bofors

RFA *Stromness*, stores support ship
Displacement: 16,792 tons full load
Speed: 18 knots
Complement: 151
Aircraft: 1 Sea King helicopter

RFA *Engadine*, helicopter support ship
Displacement: 9,000 tons full load
Complement: 77
Aircraft: 4 Wessex helicopters
          2 Wasp or 2 Sea King helicopters

Merchant Marine Ships Requisitioned for Service with the Task Force

Queen Elizabeth 2, passenger liner converted to troopship
Displacement: 67,140 tons
Owners: Cunard Steamship Co. Ltd.
Helicopter pads installed prior to sailing

Canberra, passenger liner converted to troopship
Displacement: 43,975 tons
Owners: P & O Steam Navigation Co. Ltd.
Helicopter pads installed prior to sailing

Uganda, passenger liner converted to hospital ship
Displacement: 16,910 tons
Owners: P & O Steam Navigation Co. Ltd.
Helicopter pads installed prior to sailing

Norland, passenger/vehicle ferry
Displacement: 12,990 tons
Owners: North Sea Ferries Ltd.

St Edmund, passenger/vehicle ferry
Displacement: 8,990 tons
Owners: Passtruck Shipping Co. Ltd.

Rangatira, passenger/vehicle ferry
Displacement: 8,990 tons
Owners: Passtruck Shipping Co. Ltd.

Tor Caledonia, cargo ship
Displacement: 5,060 tons
Owners: Whitwill Cole & Co. Ltd.

Elk, cargo ship
Displacement: 5,460 tons
Owners: Elk Leasing Co. Ltd.

Contender Bezant, cargo ship
Displacement: 11,445 tons
Owners: Contender 2 Ltd.

Atlantic Conveyor, cargo/container ship
Displacement: 14,950 tons
Owners: Cunard Steamship Co. Ltd.

Atlantic Causeway, cargo/container ship
Displacement: 14,950 tons
Owners: Cunard Steamship Co. Ltd.

Nordic Ferry, cargo ship/vehicle ferry
Displacement: 6,455 tons
Owners: Stena Line Ltd.

Europic Ferry, passenger/vehicle ferry
Displacement: 4,190 tons
Owners: Atlantic Steam Navigation Co. Ltd.

Baltic Ferry, cargo ship/vehicle ferry
Displacement: 6,455 tons
Owners: Stena Line Ltd.

*British Test, British Tay, British Avon, British Wye, British
Trent, British Dart, British Esk, British Tamar*, tankers
Displacement: 15,640 tons
Owners: BP Shipping Ltd./BP Thames Tanker Co. Ltd.

Balder London, tanker
Displacement: 19,980 tons
Owners: Lloyds Industrial Leasing Ltd.

Scottish Eagle, tanker
Displacement: 33,000 tons
Owners: King Line

Alvega, tanker
Displacement: 33,330 tons
Owners: Finance for Shipping Ltd.

Fort Toronto, tanker
Displacement: 19,980 tons
Owners: Canadian Pacific (Bermuda) Ltd.

Anco Charger, tanker
Displacement: 15,560 tons
Owners: P & O/Ocean Transport & Trading Ltd.

Eburna, tanker
Displacement: 19,760 tons
Owners: Shell Tankers UK Ltd.

Lycaon, cargo ship
Displacement: 11,805 tons
Owners: China Mutual Steam Navigation Co. Ltd.

Geestport, passenger/cargo ship
Displacement: 7,730 tons
Owners: Geest Industries Ltd.

St Helena, passenger/cargo ship
Displacement: 3,150 tons
Owners: United International Bank Ltd.

Saxonia, cargo ship
Displacement: 8,550 tons
Owners: Cunard Steamship Co. Ltd.

Stena Seaspread, offshore supply ship
Displacement: 6,060 tons
Owners: Stena Line Ltd.

Iris, cable ship
Displacement: 3,870 tons
Owners: British Telecom

British Enterprise III, support ship
Displacement: 1,600 tons
Owners: BUE Ships Ltd.

Cordella, Junella, Northella, Farnella, trawlers
Displacement: 1,210/1,615 tons
Owners: J. Marr

Pict, trawler
Displacement: 1,480 tons
Owners: British United Trawlers Ltd.

Yorkshireman and *Irishman*, tugs
Displacement: 690 tons
Owners: United Towing Ltd.

Salvageman, tug
Displacement: 1,600 tons
Owners: United Towing Ltd.

Wimpey Seahorse, tug
Displacement: 1,600 tons
Owners: Wimpey Marine

Ships of the Armada Republica Argentina

'SALTA' CLASS SUBMARINES

ARA *Salta*
ARA *San Luis*

Displacement: 1,185 tons surfaced
                1,285 tons submerged
Propulsion: diesel/electric
Speed submerged: 22 knots
Complement: 32
Armament: 8 × 21 inch (533 mm) torpedo tubes

These submarines were built in sections by Howaldtswerke Deutsche Werft AG of Kiel and shipped to Argentina for assembly, being commissioned in 1974. They have a reputation for quiet running when submerged, but have a rather limited endurance.

'GUPPY' CLASS SUBMARINE

ARA *Santa Fe*, ex USS *Catfish*

Displacement: 1,870 tons surfaced
                2,420 tons submerged
Propulsion: diesel/electric
Speed: 15 knots submerged
Complement: 84
Armament: 10 × 21 inch (533 mm) torpedo tubes, 6 forward
            and 4 aft

'COLOSSUS' CLASS AIRCRAFT CARRIER

ARA *Veinticinco de Mayo*, ex HrMS *Karel Doorman*, ex HMS *Venerable*

Displacement: 19,896 tons
Speed: 25 knots
Complement: 1,000
Aircraft: mixed complement of S-2E Trackers, A-4Q Sky-
hawks, Sea King ASW helicopters and A103
Alouette helicopters normally totalling 18 fixed-
wing aircraft and 4 helicopters
Guns: 10 × 40 mm

'BROOKLYN' CLASS CRUISER

ARA *General Belgrano*, formerly ARA *17 de Octubre*, ex USS
Phoenix

Displacement: 13,645 tons
Speed: 32.5 knots as new, but probably below this
Complement: 1,000
Aircraft: 2 helicopters
Missiles: 2 quad Seacat launchers
Guns: 15 × 6 inch (152 mm)
8 × 5 inch (127 mm)
2 × 40 mm
Armour: belt, 1.5–4 inches (38–102 mm)
deck, 2–3 inches (51–76 mm)
turret, 3–5 inches (76–127 mm)
control tower, 8 inches (203 mm)

TYPE 42 DESTROYERS

ARA *Hercules*
ARA *Santisima Trinidad*

Details as for British Type 42 destroyers with the following
variations:

Speed: 30 knots
Complement: 300
Missiles: 4 Exocet launchers
                   1 twin Sea Dart launcher

'FLETCHER' CLASS DESTROYERS

ARA *Rosales*, ex USS *Stembel*
ARA *Almirante Storni*, ex USS *Cowell*

Displacement: 3,050 tons
Speed: 35 knots
Complement: 249
ASW weapons: 2 Hedgehogs
                          depth charge rack
                          6 Mk 32 torpedo tubes
                          2 side-launching torpedo racks
Guns: 4 × 5 inch (127 mm)
             6 × 3 inch (76 mm)
Torpedo tubes: 4 × 21 inch (533 mm)

'ALLEN M. SUMNER' CLASS DESTROYERS

ARA *Segui*, ex USS *Hank*
ARA *Hipolito Bouchard*, ex USS *Borie*
ARA *Piedra Buena*, ex USS *Collett*

Displacement: 3,320 tons
Speed: 34 knots
Complement: 300 approx
Missiles: 4 Exocet launchers
ASW weapons: 6 Mk 32 torpedo tubes
                          2 forward-firing Hedgehogs
Guns: 6 × 5 inch (127 mm)
             4 × 3 inch (76 mm)

'GEARING' CLASS DESTROYER

ARA *Comodoro Py*, ex USS *Perkins*

Displacement: 3,500 tons
Speed: 32.5 knots
Complement: 275
Missiles: 4 Exocet launchers
ASW weapons: 6 Mk 32 torpedo tubes
            2 Hedgehogs
Guns: 6 × 5 inch (127 mm)

FRENCH TYPE A 69 CORVETTES

ARA *Drummond*
ARA *Guerrico*
ARA *Granville*

Displacement: 1,170 tons
Speed: 24 knots
Complement: 93
Missiles: 2 Exocet launchers
ASW weapons: 4 Mk 32 torpedo tubes
Guns: 1 × 3.9 inch (99 mm)
        2 × 20 mm
        2 × 40 mm

PATROL SHIPS, VARIOUS

ARA *Commandante General Irigoyen*, ex USS *Cahuilla*
ARA *Francisco de Gurruchaga*, ex USS *Luiseno*
ARA *Murature*
ARA *King*

ARA *Yamana*, ex USS *Maricopa*
ARA *Alferez Sobral*, ex USS *Catawba*
ARA *Comodoro Somellera*, ex USS *Salish*
ARA *Spiro*

These are comparatively slow vessels (12.5 to 18 knots) armed with up to six 40 mm guns; the most heavily armed are the *Murature* and *King*, which have three 4-inch (102 mm) guns, four 40 mm Bofors guns and five machine guns.

FAST ATTACK CRAFT – GUN

ARA *Intrepida*
ARA *Indomita*

Displacement: 268 tons
Speed: 40 knots
Complement: 35
Guns: 1 × 76 mm
            2 × 40 mm Bofors
Rocket launchers: 2 × 81 mm Oerlikon
Torpedo tubes: 2 × 21 inch (533 mm)

FAST ATTACK CRAFT – TORPEDO

ARA *Alakush*
ARA *Towara*

Displacement: 50 tons
Speed: 42 knots
Complement: 12
Guns: 2 × 40 mm
            4 machine guns
Rocket launchers: 2 × 8-round 127 mm

MINESWEEPERS AND MINEHUNTERS

ARA *Neuquen*, ex HMS *Hickleton*
ARA *Rio Negro*, ex HMS *Tarlton*
ARA *Chubut*, ex HMS *Santon*
ARA *Chaco*, ex HMS *Rennington*
ARA *Tierra del Fuego*, ex HMS *Bevington*
ARA *Formosa*, ex HMS *Ilmington*

Displacement: 440 tons
Speed: 15 knots
Complement: 27–36
Guns: 1 × 40 mm

ICE PATROL VESSEL

ARA *General San Martin*

Displacement: 5,301 tons
Speed: 16 knots
Complement: 160
Aircraft carried: 1 reconnaissance aircraft
                    1 helicopter
Guns: 2 × 40 mm Bofors

LANDING SHIPS, TANK

ARA *Cabo San Pio*
ARA *Cabo San Antonio*

Cabo San Antonio can carry a helicopter and is armed with
twelve 40 mm guns in three quadruple mountings. She has a
displacement of 8,000 tons fully loaded and a speed of 16
knots. *Cabo San Pio* dates from World War II, has a fully
loaded displacement of 4,080 tons and a speed of only nine
knots; she is listed as being unarmed.

TRANSPORTS

ARA *Bahia Aguirre*
ARA *Bahia Buen Suceso*
ARA *Canal Beagle*
ARA *Bahia San Blas*
ARA *Cabo de Hornos*

Bahia Aguirre and *Bahia Buen Suceso* displace 5,000 tons and have a speed of 16 knots; the remainder displace 5,800 tons and have a speed of 15 knots. None are listed as being armed.

FLEET SUPPORT TANKERS

ARA *Punta Medanos*
Displacement: 16,331 tons
Speed: 18 knots
Complement: 99

ARA *Punta Delgada*
Displacement: 6,090 tons
Speed: 11.5 knots
Complement: 72

ARA *Punta Alta*
Displacement: 1,900 tons
Speed: 8 knots
Complement: 40

II. THE ACTION

In the context of conventional warfare, the primary task of the Royal Navy today is the security of the eastern Atlantic, a task which it performs jointly with the navies of the United Kingdom's European allies. It equips, maintains and trains itself to a level above that of its likely opponent in any global war, the Soviet Navy, and since the latter has developed an extremely powerful submarine service, the Royal Navy has reacted by concentrating on all aspects of anti-submarine warfare.

Over the past 20 years two factors have changed the face of naval warfare: the nuclear reactor and the proliferation of guided weapon systems. When fitted to submarines the nuclear reactor provides them with a submerged endurance time which was undreamed of in World War II, as well as an underwater speed comparable to the majority of surface warships. Using the conventional 21-inch torpedo or the long-range guided torpedo, the nuclear-powered submarine has become the scourge not only of surface units but of its own kind, using a variety of underwater detection devices to hunt down and kill its prey from a distance. Similar devices are used to confuse the enemy's response, and the great depths to which these craft can dive provides some measure of security in itself. Understandably, the whole area of underwater electronic warfare is extremely sensitive and the most secret branch of what by tradition is known as the 'silent service' rarely reveals anything.

The Royal Navy possesses two classes of nuclear-powered hunter-killer submarines, the 'Swiftsure' and the 'Valiant' classes. It is not yet known how many submarines of this type were deployed during the Falklands Conflict, but representatives of both classes are thought to have been present up to a total of four. They did not form part of the Task Force *per se*, and their activities were controlled by the Ministry of Defence.

Their purpose was to deter, but any implied threat is meaningless unless both the means and the will to enforce it are demonstrably present. On 2 May the ARA *General Belgrano*, escorted by two destroyers, was steaming towards the edge of the Falklands' total exclusion zone, shadowed by the hunter-killer submarine HMS *Conqueror*, commanded by Commander Christopher Wreford-Brown. She was about to pass over shoal water where *Conqueror* could not follow, and since the major part of the Argentine Navy was known to be converging on the Task Force from several directions, Fleet Headquarters in London ordered *Conqueror* to sink her.

The submarine released two torpedoes – now believed to have been conventional and not the guided Tigerfish type – and these struck home on the cruiser's port side. The *General Belgrano* began to list immediately and although this was partially corrected by traversing her main armament to starboard, she continued to settle and was clearly doomed. One account suggests that her escorts fled, but *Conqueror* was subjected to a counterattack with depth charges which, as one of her petty officers was to put it, 'sounded quite close enough to me!' This the *Belgrano* was in no condition to do.

If, after this, the destroyers had quit the scene, their captains were justified in not hazarding their ships and crews by picking up survivors. The principle dated from September 1914, when Kapitan-Leutnant Weddigen of *U-9* torpedoed the cruiser HMS *Aboukir* and then sank her sister ships *Cressy* and *Hogue* while they were going to her aid. The concept that warships and trained personnel are legitimate targets, however engaged, has remained valid ever since. Wreford-Brown would have been quite entitled to sink the two destroyers if the occasion had presented itself.

In fact, such further sinkings would not have been necessary. Admiral Anaya had now lost the second largest unit of his navy before the main battle had even begun. He withdrew the remainder of his ships into Argentine territorial waters and kept them there for the duration of the conflict.

Argentina did possess three submarines of her own, but they were not the nuclear-powered hunter-killers that were now the Royal Navy's capital ships. They were small diesel/electric boats armed with conventional torpedoes but could, if given the chance, inflict serious loss on the Task Force or prey on its long supply line. One, the ARA *Santa Fe*, was damaged by air attack while running surfaced into Grytviken harbour, South Georgia, and was hastily abandoned by her crew as soon as she reached the shore. She had been carrying reinforcements for the Argentine garrison as well as its new commander, Captain Alfredo Astiz. It is possible that the *Santa Fe* might be salvaged and become a unit of the Royal Navy, but she does not fit the normal operational requirements of the British submarine service and it is more likely that she will be sold.

On 4 May one of the two surviving Argentine submarines launched an unsuccessful torpedo attack on the Task Force, and may have been sunk or seriously damaged by a Sea King's Stringray torpedo. Nonetheless, Admiral Woodward could not ignore the submarine factor. It would, for example, have given Argentina's morale a tremendous lift if the *Queen Elizabeth 2* had been torpedoed and sunk. In fact, the *Queen Elizabeth 2* did not enter the Falklands battle zone; instead, she trans-shipped the 5th Infantry Brigade off South Georgia and returned home with the survivors of HMS *Sheffield*, *Coventry*, *Ardent* and *Antelope*.

In the few years between the demise of the battleship and the birth of the nuclear submarine, it was the aircraft carrier which was regarded as the capital ship of the world's navies. It is still of supreme importance, for no naval undertaking, amphibious or otherwise, can succeed unless adequate air cover is present. One of the great ironies of the Falklands conflict is that had Argentina waited several months before launching its invasion, Great Britain would have been unable to mount a credible response, for *Hermes* was bound for the breaker's yard and *Invincible* was to have joined the Royal Australian Navy. The Royal Navy would have been left with one 'Invincible' class light carrier still being fitted out and one elderly commando carrier, HMS *Bulwark*, in reserve; in other words, with no operational carriers at all.

This was an area in which the defence economists' axe had played havoc. Large aircraft carriers such as HMS *Ark Royal*, capable of launching and recovering conventional fixed-wing jet aircraft, had been phased out because they were said to be too vulnerable. This was not a view supported by the United States Navy, which maintains a number of large carrier groups, nor is it immediately clear why a light carrier should be any the less vulnerable. The truth is that the Treasury could not or would not support the cost of running large aircraft carriers and because of this Great Britain was all but caught short in the strategic sense and actually caught short in a number of tactical areas.

Hermes, the flagship of the Task Force, went to battle with one engine temporarily out of commission; she was to suffer machinery problems throughout the campaign. She was built as a conventional carrier and still possesses the angled flight deck which had once enabled her to launch and recover aircraft simultaneously, but her steam catapults and arrester gear have long since been stripped out. During her normal role as anti-submarine warfare/commando carrier her complement of aircraft is five Sea Harriers and nine Sea King helicopters, but this was effectively doubled when she left for the South Atlantic, taking up every spare inch. Whatever her age or defects, *Hermes* was the lynch-pin of the Task Force and without her its job would have bordered on the impossible.

Invincible, Admiral Woodward's second carrier, is a much younger ship and had been in commission for less than two years when the conflict started. She has a straight-through flight deck terminating short of the bows in a 'ski-jump' which is designed to give her Sea Harriers extra lift during their short take-off; this feature is rather less pronounced than that fitted to *Hermes*. The first of a class intended to number three, *Invincible* is easily recognisable by her two funnels. In normal times she carries five Sea Harriers and ten Sea King helicopters but, like *Hermes*, she carried twice that number during the conflict.

Argentina's only carrier, the *Veinticinco de Mayo*, is even older than *Hermes*, and has seen previous service in the Royal Navy and the Royal Netherlands Navy. She is, however, a conventional carrier with an angled flight deck, steam catapults and arrester gear, and can launch 18 Skyhawks and a number of helicopters. There is no doubt that her aircraft flew numerous sorties, but after she had covered the invasion of the Falklands, *Veinticinco de Mayo* is known to have had machinery problems and, following the sinking of the *General*

Belgrano, she was kept out of the conflict.

It is possible that a few veterans of the first Battle of the Falklands in 1914, now octogenarians, watched the ships of the Task Force going down-Channel to round Ushant; it is certain that many veterans of the River Plate action in 1939 did so. It would, perhaps, have seemed strange to them that whereas their own ships had bristled with guns, Admiral Woodward's destroyers and frigates mounted so very few. The majority of ships carried one or two 4.5-inch (114 mm) guns in a single turret, their only other conventional armament being a few 20 mm Oerlikon and 40 mm Bofors guns for close air defence. The gun, in fact, has become a secondary weapon system, although the Vickers 4.5-inch is fully automated and can pump out one round every two seconds with impressive accuracy.

The real teeth of the Royal Navy's surface fleet lies partially concealed in unimpressive box-like launchers, for the missile has a longer range than the gun and is more reliable and devastating in its effects. The missiles in service with the Task Force included the surface-skimming anti-ship Exocet MM.38, the Seaslug anti-aircraft missile, which also provides an anti-ship potential, the Sea Dart long-range and Seacat short-range anti-aircraft missiles, the formidable Seawolf surface-to-air missile which can be used either against aircraft or incoming missiles and which has been known to intercept shells in flight, and the Ikara long-range homing torpedo launch vehicle. Different ships carried different mixes of weapon systems and it was thus necessary to balance the composition of any group to cover as many offensive and defensive options as possible.

The missile has brought about a revolution in warship design. Early warning, target acquisition and guidance radar scanners all have to be mounted as high as possible to provide the necessary wide horizon. This means that the warship has a tall silhouette and is burdened with a great deal of top-hamper, giving a high centre of gravity. Simultaneously, advances in technology have resulted in smaller, lighter main engines, thus aggravating the problem. Heavy armour plate, which once protected hulls against shellfire and which also kept the centre of gravity low, provides no defence at all against the missile's shaped-charge warhead, and its incorporation in warship design has long been abandoned. The equation was finally solved by building upper works in lightweight aluminium instead of the more usual steel.

During the conflict, much was made of the fact that aluminium has a lower melting point than steel. This is true, but at that temperature destruction tends to be total anyway. The characteristics of aluminium had been known for some time, in fact since a serious fire gutted an American warship off Vietnam; in this incident a number of men lost their lives, unable to reach safety because aluminium companionways had melted. The Royal Navy insisted that its companionways should continue to be made of steel.

A sophisticated electronic environment such as a missile-armed warship contains many miles of cable, and it was the insulation for this, together with a number of other plastic components, which proved to be the real ship-killer. Once a serious fire had broken out, the interior of the vessel filled with such dense black smoke that it was impossible either to see or to breathe. Consequently, damage control parties were unable to carry out their work and the ship continued to consume herself. It is understood that these defects are to be remedied.

Again, the very nature of electronic warfare means that in action a warship is no longer commanded from her bridge. Instead, operations are conducted from a control room containing radar and weapon system consoles, located within the superstructure. In this context it should be mentioned that existing Royal Navy designs were finalised before surface-skimming missiles such as Exocet had entered general service, for Exocet flies at control-room height and it was in this area that HMS *Sheffield* was hit on 4 May; even had she not become a total loss her potential as a fighting unit would have been destroyed. It is no secret that the Royal Navy had not expected to find itself at war with an enemy armed with NATO weapons, or that the Soviet Union is still some years behind the West in the field of surface-skimming missiles.

The normal electronic countermeasure to an incoming missile is for chaff – a bundle of the thin metal foil strips known in World War II as Window – to be fired from a mortar. This is intended to inject confusing images into the missile's radar brain so that the missile itself is drawn harmlessly above and behind the target vessel. Some evidence suggests that Exocet is not greatly influenced by chaff.

Deadly though Exocet might be when it strikes, adding its remaining fuel to the inferno caused by the explosion of its warhead inside the target, it is not invulnerable and can be destroyed by the Seawolf system, provided its approach has been detected early enough. It can also be destroyed by the American Vulcan air defence system, which has been available since the Vietnam war and is small enough to be mounted on a tracked armoured personnel carrier. In simple terms, the Vulcan is a six-barrelled machine gun which operates on the revolving Gatling principle. It can produce an output of 6,000 rounds per minute, but is normally governed below this level. The naval version, named Vulcan/Phalanx, has been matched to a guidance radar set and is fitted to major US Navy ships as a close-range defence against missiles. During practice firings it has produced some impressive results against faster flying targets than Exocet. No warship within the Task Force was fitted with this weapon system in spite of the fact that it was available and that it had a relevant application; the Ministry of Defence has subsequently purchased several Vulcan systems.

A further area in which the Task Force fought at a disadvantage stemmed from the absence of an airborne warning and control system (AWACS). The advantages of such a system are obvious. Masthead radar can see only as far as the natural horizon and in a straight line beyond, but a suitable set mounted in a high-flying aircraft can see beyond the curvature of the earth's surface and give advance warning of intruders long before they become visible on screens at sea level. The United States Air Force already has an operational AWACS aircraft in the Boeing E-3A Sentry but this could not be involved because, although the American government was supplying material assistance to the United Kingdom, Sentry could only have entered the battle zone manned by US personnel, and that would have compromised the American stance of neutrality. The Royal Air Force is well advanced in the development of its own AWACS, using an adapted British Aerospace Nimrod, but this is not due to enter service until 1983. It was yet another irony that the Fleet Air Arm's Gannet aircraft *had* provided a rudimentary but acceptable form of AWACS, but they had been phased out along with the big aircraft carriers. Even if an airworthy Gannet could have been found and fitted out it could not have been used, since it had to be launched by steam catapult and such equipment did not exist within the Task Force.

The Argentine Navy had its problems, too. It is essentially a coastal defence force and even following the invasion of the Falklands it was necessary for it to return to its bases for fuel and supplies. It cannot maintain itself in open water for long, whereas the Royal Navy does so as a matter of routine, using the tankers, supply ships and support vessels of the Royal Fleet Auxiliary Service.

It was, therefore, with these various factors in mind and in the full knowledge that, initially at least, he had only 20 Sea Harriers at his disposal, that Admiral Woodward had to plan his strategy. The risks remained very grave, even after the Argentine navy had retired from the contest.

In the event, Woodward deployed the main body of the Task Force at the approximate limit of the FAA's fuel endurance, ensuring that any contact was of limited duration only. To compensate for the lack of an AWACS he was forced to position individual ships forward of the fleet to act as radar pickets and provide some early warning of the enemy's intentions. It was in this role that HMS *Sheffield* and, later, HMS *Coventry* were lost.

Much careful consideration was given to the choice of a suitable beachhead for the amphibious landing, without which the operation could not be concluded, for this would see the Task Force at its moment of greatest risk. A sheltered anchorage and a beach across which vehicles and supplies could pass were prime requirements. The broken outer coastline of the islands did offer some possibilities but these were highly exposed to the rising winter gales; Falkland Sound, on the other hand, offered ideal geographic facilities, but against this it was a narrow stretch of water which constrained manoeuvre. Many believed that Admiral Woodward intended to land on West Falkland, which was known to be lightly defended, and he did nothing to correct that belief. Such a landing would undoubtedly have succeeded, although it would have prolonged the conflict. The inflexible rule in the conduct of any war is that it is the main mass of the enemy's force which has to be defeated; that mass was present on East Falkland, and since the British commander was aiming for a quick victory, it was on East Falkland that the landing would have to be made.

One thing was clear from the outset – given the number of troops at General Menendez' disposal, he could not be strong everywhere. The reports coming back from SAS and SBS teams already operating on East Falkland confirmed that the Argentines were strong nowhere save at Port Stanley and Goose Green; Falkland Sound was barely defended at all. Woodward promptly selected the sheltered San Carlos Water, an inlet off the Sound, which also had the advantage of placing the beachhead beyond the reach of a major counter-attack by the enemy's ground troops. A further factor for consideration was that the overwhelming strength of the FAA had not yet been written down to a safe level, and for this reason a night landing was ordered.

The assembly of the landing force and its escorts at sea was again an organisational triumph. Men, tanks, missiles, guns and ammunition had to come off in the right order and be fully protected while they did so. The landing itself took place during the night of 20/21 May and a beachhead was established against only a token opposition; the only casualties incurred were those caused by accident.

If the reaction of the Argentine army was barely noticed, that of the FAA was violent in the extreme. Waves of Mirages and Skyhawks came in from the mainland, flying low and using the Falklands land mass to minimise radar detection. Sweeping down over the low hills they strafed the ships with their cannon, fired rockets and released bombs. Piston-engined Pucaras, flying from Falklands air strips, joined in the fray. From the warships and the beachhead missiles rose to meet them, locking on to their exhaust wakes and chasing them to destruction as they banked for the cover of high ground, their bombs and ammunition expended; in some instances missile met missile to detonate in a thunderous mid-air explosion.

For many aboard the ships the most comforting sounds were those of a much earlier war: the sustained rattle of the Oerlikons and the steady thump of the Bofors. Light general-purpose machine guns were mounted wherever possible, putting up a curtain of lead through which the enemy had to fly; as a defence against low-level attack this has always been effective and on this occasion, too, it was to score kills.

Some, like those manning the landing craft or the personnel of the Royal Corps of Transport and the Royal Engineers manning their own watercraft, could not hit back but continued with their work, which at least occupied their minds. Others, particularly aboard the merchant ships detailed to accompany the landing force, could only watch. From the air the 44,000-ton *Canberra*, known to the troops as 'The Great White Whale', must have dominated the scene, but she emerged from her ordeal unscathed. The crew of the *Europic Ferry*, too, felt at a disadvantage since their ship was painted a brilliant orange that was intended to attract business. She was now, they felt, attracting the wrong sort of business and they plastered her hull with a selection of home-made grey paints. The result was anything but harmonious but *Europic* arrived home intact.

With one notable break, the FAA continued to press home its attacks with determination and courage in spite of the mounting carnage being inflicted on its pilots and aircraft. The British, too, had their losses. The Type 21 frigate *Ardent* became a particular target and was hit again and again by rockets. Despite the efforts of John Leake, her civilian canteen manager who used a machine gun against the Argentine aircraft, and of many men like him, *Ardent* was a dying ship and eventually went down, taking her 22 dead with her.

Other ships were riddled with cannon fire and hit by bombs. Captain Christopher Layman's *Argonaut*, a 'Leander' class frigate, was first strafed by Pucaras and then became the target of six Skyhawks. She shot down one of her attackers but two bombs struck her, neither exploding. The first ripped its way into the engine room below the water line, putting the engines and steering gear out of action; the second passed through a fuel tank into the forward magazine, starting an ammunition fire and causing explosions which killed two men. Layman dealt with the fire by flooding the magazine with diesel oil. *Argonaut*, dead in the water, was towed to an anchorage and went on fighting, downing a second Skyhawk. It was 24 hours before the bomb in her engine room was defused, but six days before that in her magazine was made safe. During that time she remained in action against the FAA and was then patched up sufficiently to enable her to limp back to the United Kingdom at 10 knots.

HMS *Antrim*, which had played a major part in the recovery of South Georgia, had a miraculous escape. A bomb smashed its way through the rear missile flash door, passed through the aft magazine and lodged in the heads. It took ten hours work to defuse it, work it free and toss it over the side. *Antelope*, the twin sister of HMS *Ardent*, was not so lucky. She had already been damaged when her engine room was penetrated by a bomb which detonated while an explosives officer was working on it. Fire raged throughout the ship, which eventually had to be abandoned. When the flames reached her magazines *Antelope* exploded and sank, her back broken.

This first phase of the air-sea battle ended on 25 May with the sinking of HMS *Coventry* and the *Atlantic Conveyor*. During the attack on *Coventry* the destroyer *Broadsword* had also been struck by a bomb which bounced off the water, passed through her side and then left the ship via the flight deck, wrecking her helicopter. It has been suggested that the *Atlantic Conveyor* became the target of an Exocet missile because her radar profile was very similar to that of the British aircraft carriers. Her smoking hulk remained afloat for several days and Argentine propaganda was more than usually insistent that the carrier *Invincible* had been crippled. The *Atlantic Conveyor* had ferried a score of Harriers into the battle zone, but they had flown off some time before she was struck. Her legacy is to demonstrate that the use of long-hulled container vessels as temporary carriers for V/STOL aircraft is a viable proposition, and the idea is to be developed further.

Admiral Woodward had already stated that he expected to lose five naval units, one of them of major importance. His forecast thus far had been remarkably accurate, but to the debit column must be added *Argonaut* and *Glasgow* ordered home for repairs, the latter damaged when a bomb had passed straight through her hull from side to side on 12 May, off Port Stanley. Offset against these losses were the reinforcements which were arriving, so that the Task Force was now actually stronger than when it had first gone into action.

The battle in Falkland Sound marked a turning point in the history of air-sea warfare. Ever since the Fleet Air Arm crippled the Italian Navy at Taranto in 1940, when air and sea power have met it has been the former which prevailed. Off Crete in 1941 the Royal Navy found itself in direct confrontation with the Luftwaffe, whose crack dive-bomber squadrons pressed home their attacks with determination and vigour. Altogether, the Navy's losses totalled three cruisers and eight destroyers sunk, the latter including the late Lord Mountbatten's *Kelly*, and three battleships, one carrier, seven cruisers and nine destroyers damaged, some very seriously. The loss of life was terrible, 725 dying on the cruiser *Gloucester* alone. All this the Luftwaffe achieved at the cost of a handful of aircraft. The lessons of Crete were repeated throughout World War II. Off Malaya the *Prince of Wales* and *Repulse* fell victim to Japanese air power. During the vital battle of Midway the opposing fleets never even sighted each other, all damage being inflicted by aircraft. Until the Falklands War, nothing that has happened since has done anything to alter the view that aircraft have the advantage over ships.

But in Falkland Sound the Royal Navy's gun line not only held while the beachhead was consolidated but its weapon systems, aided by those of the troops ashore and the Harriers fighting their interception battle out at sea, inflicted catastrophic losses on the FAA. Considering the size of the undertaking, remarkably few British ships and lives were lost.

It can be argued that British losses would have been much heavier had all the enemy's bombs exploded. They did not explode because, as we shall see, the FAA chose to attack in a certain way; this was not induced by the enclosed nature of the Sound, for it chose to employ the same technique for attacks in open water. The ships themselves were severely constrained in the degree of evasive action which they could take. Whichever way one looks at it, the battle of Falkland Sound was a clear-cut naval victory.

Following the break-out from the beachhead the focus of attention turned to the land battle, while the Royal Navy stepped up its bombardment of targets in the Port Stanley area.

It was the discovery that General Menendez had withdrawn his troops from Fitzroy that involved the Royal Navy in a second assault landing, this time at Bluff Cove. This operation had to be mounted quickly and was carried out by the logistic landing ships *Sir Galahad* and *Sir Tristram*. Anchored offshore, the ships were easy targets for the FAA, which now returned briefly but vigorously to the battle. Both were hit, but while *Sir Tristram* eventually brought her fires under control, *Sir Galahad*'s were beyond containment. Hundreds of troops were still aboard, as well as tons of ammunition and fuel. Fifty men died in that holocaust of flames, explosions and stifling black smoke. If one lesson stands out beyond others, it is that in these circumstances disembarkation of personnel must hold priority above other considerations, for even when subjected to air attack men on the ground are less at risk than men concentrated aboard ship. Bluff Cove contained the elements of disaster but it achieved its object. The lives lost must be balanced against those saved in shortening the war by several days. When the FAA, encouraged by its success, came back later that same day it fared no better than it had in Falkland Sound.

While the attacks on Bluff Cove were taking place the FAA did, in fact, return to the Sound, singling out HMS *Plymouth* as its target. Two aircraft were shot down but the frigate was struck by four bombs in rapid succession. One passed through her funnel, two more wrecked an anti-submarine mortar before making their exit through the ship's side, while the fourth struck a depth charge, starting a serious fire. It took 50 minutes to bring the situation under control and for a while *Plymouth*'s future hung in the balance.

On the night of 12 June the 3rd Commando Brigade

launched a successful offensive against enemy positions around Port Stanley, warships providing direct fire support as follows: HMS *Avenger* for 3rd Battalion, The Parachute Regiment on Mount Longdon, HMS *Glamorgan* for 45 Commando on the Two Sisters, HMS *Yarmouth* for 42 Commando on Mount Harriet, and HMS *Arrow* for the SAS squadron operating in the Murrel Hills. Each 4.5 inch gun produced the equivalent output per minute as one of the Royal Artillery's six-gun 105 mm light gun batteries, five of which were already firing on the same targets. During these operations HMS *Glamorgan* was hit by an Exocet missile launched from the shore; she sustained casualties and damage but survived, being the sixteenth, and last, British warship to be damaged by enemy action.

The Royal Navy had seen active service during the Korean War, the Suez Crisis and the Indonesian Confrontation, but the Falklands Conflict was its first major battle since 1945 and, incidentally, the first three-dimensional missile war in naval history. Many lessons had been learned – and not a few taught – and the design of its ships and those of other navies will profit by them, particularly in the area of damage control and the provision of a satisfactory weapon balance.

Like many Latin American navies, the Armada Republica Argentina enjoys the prestige conferred by a display of weapons on the upper decks of its warships, hence the large number of gun-armed ex-American destroyers in service, some of which have recently been fitted with Exocet missile launchers. Nonetheless, these are becoming elderly and are slowly being replaced with modern warships built in British or European yards.

The Argentine armed services had not fought a foreign enemy for the best part of a century and although their theoretical training was thorough they gave the impression of being unaware of the fearful effects of modern weapons at close quarters. This first became apparent during their invasion of South Georgia when one of its navy's new French-built Type A 69 corvettes, either *Drummond* or *Guerrico*, sailed into Grytviken harbour in support of the helicopter landing which was already taking place. She entered in the grand manner, as though under sail, hoping to intimidate the tiny Royal Marine garrison. The Marines, at 200 yards (183 m) range, blew a hole in her water line with an 84 mm anti-tank missile, and a further hole in her superstructure with a 66 mm anti-tank rocket, hoping to knock out the control room. A second 84 mm round hit the Exocet launcher but failed to explode; she was also struck by 1,000 rounds of small-arms ammunition. Badly knocked about, the corvette rapidly reversed course and limped out to sea. The lesson was elementary – in real war one should neither underestimate one's opponents, nor their weapons.

On the same day that the *Belgrano* was torpedoed, the Prefectura Naval Argentina's two patrol craft in the Falklands, *Rio Iguazu* and *Islas Malvinas*, were engaged by Task Force helicopters while searching for lost aircrew. The former was sunk and the latter, slightly damaged, was driven ashore and abandoned. Repaired, she was manned by personnel from HMS *Cardiff*, renamed *Tiger Bay* and is still on station. On 3 May the remaining vessels of the Argentine inshore squadron, the gunboats *Comodoro Somellera* and *Alferez Sobral*, emerged to look for survivors from the patrol craft and initiated an engagement with Task Force helicopters which replied with Sea Skua missiles. The *Comodoro Somellera* was sunk but the *Alferez Sobral* managed to stagger back to the mainland, almost a total wreck.

There was certainly no lack of courage among Argentine seamen. Supply ships, manned by naval personnel or volunteer crews, continued in their attempts to run the blockade throughout the war. One got through only days before General Menendez surrendered; two, the *Islas de Los Estados* and the *Rio Carcarania*, paid the ultimate price for their daring.

Nor was the Argentine navy lacking in brave and intelligent officers who must have felt bitterly resentful at being confined to their own coastal waters. For Admiral Anaya, the preservation of his fleet held vital political as well as service considerations. His actions may have earned him the dislike of his fellows within the junta but, perversely, they did not lead to his disgrace. He could, with some justice, plead that the navy's losses were proportionate to those of the other armed services.

2

The air battle – helicopters

I. THE HARDWARE

AGUSTA A109A

Designation: multi-role helicopter
Engines: 2 × 420 shp (313 kW) Allison 250–C20B
            turboshafts
Maximum speed at sea level: 165 mph (266 km/h)
Range at sea level: 351 miles (565 km)
Capacity: pilot, co-pilot and 6 fully equipped troops
Armament: 1 remotely sighted and aimed machine gun
             2 rocket pods or 4 TOW or HOT missiles

In service with: Argentina.

One captured example was returned to the United Kingdom
and has been taken into service with the Royal Navy.

AÉROSPATIALE ALOUETTE III

Designation: general-purpose helicopter
Engine: 1 governed 870 shp (649 kW), Turboméca Astazou
           turboshaft
Maximum speed at sea level: 136 mph (218 km/h)
Maximum rate of climb at sea level: 885 ft (270 m)/minute
Range at sea level: 375 miles (600 km)
Capacity: pilot and 6 fully equipped troops
Armament: (light assault helicopter) 1 light or medium
             machine gun
             guided air-to-ground missiles
             rocket pod
             (ASW role) 1 homing torpedo
             2 air-to-surface guided missiles

In service with: Armada Republica Argentina

AÉROSPATIALE/WESTLAND GAZELLE

Designation: multi-role utility helicopter
Engine: 1 × 590 shp (440 kW) Turboméca Astazou
        turboshaft
Maximum speed at sea level: 193 mph (311 km/h)
Maximum rate of climb at sea level: 1,770 ft (540 m)/
                                        minute
Range at sea level: 223 miles (359 km)
Capacity: (normal) pilot, co-pilot and 3 passengers
           (casualty evacuation) pilot, 2 stretcher cases, 1
           medical orderly
           (cargo) 1,540 lbs (699 kg) slung
Armament: 4 × AS.11 or 2 × AS.12
           4 or 6 HOT guided anti-tank missiles
           2 × 7.62 mm forward-firing machine guns
           or 2 × 68 mm rocket pods
In service with: Royal Navy
                   Royal Air Force
                   Army Air Corps

The Gazelle was originally developed for the French Army as
a replacement for the Alouette, the project later attracting
British participation. In the British Army of the Rhine the
machine serves as a light observation helicopter with an anti-
tank capability and equips one of the Army Air Corps' two
divisional helicopter squadrons, the other being equipped
with the Lynx. An unusual feature is the 'fenestron' or
shrouded tail rotor.

AÉROSPATIALE/WESTLAND SA 330 PUMA

Designation: medium transport helicopter
Engines: 2 × 1,575 shp (1,175 kW) Turboméca Turmo
          IVC turboshafts
Maximum speed at sea level: 182 mph (293 km/h)
Maximum rate of climb at sea level: 1,810 ft (552 m)/
                                        minute

Range at sea level: 355 miles (571 km/h)
Capacity: (assault) 16/20 fully equipped troops
(casualty evacuation) 6 stretchers, 6 seated
wounded
(cargo carrier) 5,511 lbs (2,502 kg) slung
Armament: various, including side-firing 20 mm cannon
axial 7.62 mm machine guns
rockets
missiles

In service with: Royal Air Force
Armada Republica Argentina

The Puma can also serve as a fire support helicopter. RAF
versions have a rescue hoist fitted as standard equipment.

BELL UH-1N

Designation: multi-role utility and transport helicopter
Engine: Pratt & Whitney 1,290 shp (962 kW) PT6T-3
Twin-Pac turboshaft
Maximum speed at sea level: 161 mph (259 km)
Range at sea level: 261 miles (420 km)
Capacity: pilot and 14 fully equipped infantrymen or 6
stretcher cases
Armament: homing torpedoes
depth charges
air-to-surface missiles

In service with: Armada Republica Argentina

1. The Task Force sails south to the Falkland Islands

2. HMS *Hermes*, the Task Force flagship

3. Two able seamen in the operations room of HMS *Invincible* maintaining contact with escorting ships

4. HMS *Invincible*

5. HMS *Endurance* and HMS *Plymouth* in Leith Harbour, South Georgia

6. HMS *Conqueror*, the nuclear-powered submarine which sank the *General Belgrano*

7.   HMS *Spartan*, one of the 'Swiftsure' class of hunter-killer submarines

8. Type 42 destroyer HMS *Sheffield* after being hit by Argentine Exocet missile on 4 May

9. HMS *Broadsword*, one of the Type 22 frigates armed with the Seawolf missile

10. 'County' class destroyer HMS *Antrim*

11. *Sheffield*'s sister ship HMS *Coventry* which was sunk on 25 May off the northern entrance to Falkland Sound

12. HMS *Plymouth*, a modified Type 12 frigate

13. HMS *Antelope* with its back broken in Falkland Sound

14. HMS *Arrow*, the Type 21 frigate which took off survivors from *Sheffield*

15. Assault ship HMS *Fearless*

16. Royal Fleet Auxiliary tanker refuelling *Canberra* in South Atlantic

17. HMS *Sir Tristram*, the logistic landing ship badly damaged in the air attack at Bluff Cove

18.   HMS *Sir Galahad* ablaze in Bluff Cove

19.   Bombs exploding around MV *Norland* in San Carlos Water

20. Sea King helicopter with anti-submarine sonar suspended in the sea

21. Sea King helicopter landing troops on Task Force carrier

22. Wessex helicopter

23. Scout helicopter

24. Argentine Mirage fighter dodging anti-aircraft fire from British ships

25. Sea Harrier aboard HMS *Hermes*

26. Sea Harriers landing on HMS *Invincible*

27. RAF Vulcan

28. Cluster bomb releasing its sub-munitions

29. Port Stanley airfield showing bomb-damaged Pucara aircraft and buildings

30. Destroyed Argentine Pucara

31. RAF Nimrod which performed maritime reconnaissance from Ascension Island

32. Marine test-firing LAW anti-tank weapon from *Canberra* en route to Falkland Islands

33. Marines from 42 Commando leave *Canberra* on landing craft in San Carlos Water

34. 3-ton, 1-ton and ¼-ton transports being ferried ashore at San Carlos

35. Royal Engineers' equipment being landed at San Carlos. Wheeled tractor in fore is laying flexible trackway across beach

36. Centurion beach armoured recovery vehicle (BARV)

37.   Marines firing an 81 mm mortar on Ascension Island

38.   FV 180 combat engineer tractor

39. Air defence gunner at San Carlos

40. AML-90 light armoured car of the type used by Argentines on Falkland Islands

41. Scorpion light tanks of the Blues and Royals on Falklands

42.   LVTP-7 of the type which Argentines used to occupy Port Stanley

43.   British troops digging in on Falklands

44. Royal Marines with Snowcats

45. 105 mm light gun emplacement in action

46. British troops advancing over hills above Port Stanley

47. Gurkhas with captured Argentine Rheinmetall 20 mm anti-aircraft gun

48. British troops inspecting Argentine Oerlikon 35 mm twin anti-aircraft gun

49. Seawolf anti-missile and anti-aircraft missile being fired

50. Exocet surface-to-surface missile

51. British Seaslug missile

52. Sea Dart missile launcher

53. Rapier anti-aircraft missile battery overlooking San Carlos Water

54. Harriers and helicopters on HMS *Hermes*

55. Soldier with Blowpipe missile launcher at San Carlos

BOEING-VERTOL CH-47 CHINOOK

Designation: tandem-rotor medium transport helicopter
Engines: 2 × 3,750 shp (2,796 kW) Lycoming T55-L-11C
            turboshafts
Maximum speed at sea level: 189 mph (304 km/h)
Maximum rate of climb at sea level: 2,880   ft   (878   m)/
                                                    minute
Range at sea level: 1,331 miles (2,142 km)
                      (Argentina's   Type   308:   1,265   miles
                      (2,036km)
Capacity: (troop transport) 44 seats
            (casualty evacuation) 24 stretcher cases
            (cargo carrier) hooks, front and rear, 20,000 lbs
            (9,072 kg) each
            hook, centre, 28,000 lbs (12,712 kg)
Armament: normally none

In service with: Royal Air Force
                   Argentina (Type 308 specially adapted for
                   logistic support and rescue operations in
                   Antarctica)

WESTLAND/AÉROSPATIALE LYNX

Designation: (AH 1 military version) general purpose tac-
               tical helicopter
               (HAS 2 naval version) shipboard ASW and
               anti-ship search, strike and reconnaissance
               helicopter
Engines: 2 × 1,120 shp (835 kW) Rolls-Royce Gem 41-1
            turboshafts
Maximum speed at sea level: 200 mph (322 km/h)
Maximum rate of climb at sea level: 2,180 ft (664 m)/
                                                minute
Range with full payload at sea level: 336 miles (541 km)
Capacity: (troop carrier) 10 men

Armament: (AH 1) 8 HOT or TOW or 6 AS.11 anti-tank
            guided weapons
            minigun with 3,000 rounds in ventral turret
            1 × 20 mm cannon in cabin or 2 × 20 mm
            cannon on external mountings
            1 × 7.62 mm machine gun in cabin
            rocket pods
            (HAS 2) 2 homing torpedoes or 2 depth
            charges
            4 Sea Skua or AS.12 air-to-surface missiles

In service with: Royal Navy
                   Army Air Crops
                   Armada Republica Argentina

The Lynx was designed by Westland Helicopters but is
manufactured jointly with Aérospatiale of France, the latter
having a 30 per cent holding. Quite apart from the very wide
range of attack stores that can be carried, it is also one of the
most versatile combat rotocraft ever built and can reach a
speed of 230 mph (370 km/h) when diving, fly backward at 80
mph (129 km/h) and roll at 100 degrees per second. The AH 1
has begun to replace the Scout in Army Air Corps squadrons
in West Germany, while the HAS 2 is to replace the Wasp in
naval service.

   The AH 1 has been designed to integrate fully within a land
battle and can perform a variety of roles including anti-tank,
armed escort, sensor reconnaissance, command post, casualty
evacuation and general transport. The HAS 2 is equipped
with dunking sonar for submarine detection and can also
perform the search and rescue role, being equipped with a
winch for the recovery of survivors.

WESTLAND SCOUT AND WASP

Designation: (Scout) multi-role tactical helicopter
               (Wasp) general-purpose and ASW helicopter
               for use from small vessels

Engines: (Scout) 1 × 685 shp (511 kW) Rolls-Royce
Nimbus 102 turboshaft
(Wasp) 1 × 710 shp (530 kW) Rolls-Royce
Nimbus 103 turboshaft
Maximum speed at sea level: (Scout) 131 mph (211 km/h)
(Wasp) 120 mph (193 km/h)
Maximum rate of climb at sea level: (Scout) 1,670 ft (509
m)/minute
(Wasp) 1,440 ft (439
m)/minute)
Range at sea level: (Scout) 315 miles (507 km)
(Wasp) 270 miles (435 km)
Capacity: 2 crew and 4 passengers
Armament: aimed automatic weapons up to 20 mm calibre
fixed general-purpose machine gun mountings
rocket pods or guided missiles
Wasp can also carry homing torpedoes

In service with: (Scout) Army Air Corps
(Wasp) Royal Navy

WESTLAND SEA KING

Designation: amphibious all-weather ASW, search-and-
rescue, tactical military or general-purpose
helicopter
Engines: 2 Rolls-Royce Gnome 1,660 shp (1,238 kW)
turboshaft
Maximum speed at sea level: 143 mph (230 km/h)
Maximum rate of climb at sea level: 2,020 ft (616 m)/
minute
Range at sea level: 764 miles (1,230 km)
Capacity: (troop carrier) 22 men
(casualty evacuation) 6 stretcher cases and 12
seated wounded
(cargo) 6,500 lbs (2,951 kg) slung externally
Armament: various, including automatic weapons, rocket
pods, missiles and homing torpedoes

In service with: Royal Air Force
                   Royal Navy

The Sea King is an advanced development of the Sikorsky S-61 Sea King – of which Argentina owns several – and is built under licence in the United Kingdom by Westland Helicopters. The ASW version can be distinguished by its radome and employs dunking sonar in conjunction with a number of efficient search-and-destroy electronic systems.

WESTLAND WESSEX

Designation: multi-role helicopter
Engines: 1 Rolls-Royce Gazelle 161, 162 or 165 with respective shp of 1,450 (1,082 kW), 1,540 (1,149 kW) and 1,600 (1,194 kW)
or, 2 Rolls-Royce coupled Gnomes Marks 112 and 113 with a combined power of 1,550 shp (1,156 kW)
Maximum speed at sea level: 133 mph (214 km/h)
Maximum rate of climb at sea level: 1,650 ft (503 m)/minute
Capacity: (troop carrier) 16 men
(casualty evacuation) 7 stretcher cases
(cargo) 4,000 lbs (1,816 kg)
Armament: various, including 2 × 7.62 mm general-purpose machine guns or 20 mm cannon
rocket pods or 4 missiles
ASW versions carry one or two homing torpedoes

In service with: Royal Navy
                   Royal Marines
                   Royal Air Force

An improved version of the Sikorsky S-58 manufactured under licence by Westland Helicopters. ASW models have a pronounced radome behind the rotor. The RAF's HC2 model has coupled Gnome engines.

WESTLAND WHIRLWIND

Designation: light utility helicopter
Engine: 1 × 1,050 shp (783 kW) Rolls-Royce Gnome
         H.1000 turboshaft
Maximum speed at sea level: 106 mph (171 km/h)
Range at sea level: 300 miles (483 km)
Capacity: (troop carrier) 8/10 men
           (casualty evacuation) 6 stretcher cases and
           medical orderly
Arament: normally none

In service with: Royal Navy
                  Army Air Corps
                  Royal Air Force
                  Argentine services

The Whirlwind is based on the Sikorsky S-55 and built under
licence by Westland Aircraft.

II. THE ACTION

The helicopter was first employed on a substantial scale during the Korean War, when the United States Army used large numbers for casualty evacuation. Since then, both the size of helicopters and the scope of their activities have been expanded to such proportions that no country dare ignore its helicopter arm, which adds what might be described as a fourth dimension to the land and sea battle.

In so far as the land battle is concerned, the tasks of the helicopter fleet may be summarised as follows: overall surveillance of the battlefield; concentration of superior forces at the point of contact; destruction of the enemy's armour; suppression of the enemy's defensive fire; deep penetration operations in the enemy's rear; the insertion of special forces, such as the SAS, into sensitive areas; interference with the enemy's transport and supply elements; and disruption of the enemy's battlefield electronic equipment by jamming.

In this context the majority of combat helicopters fall into three types: attack, assault troop carrier, and supply. The attack helicopter, or gunship, carries a wide variety of armaments for close support of the ground troops, including cannon, machine guns, rockets and anti-tank guided weapons (ATGW). The assault troop carrier can carry one or more fully equipped infantry sections, dropping them within easy striking distance of their objective and then, if required, lifting them out when their mission has been completed. The supply helicopter is designed for the bulk forward delivery of ammunition and stores, but can also double as a troop carrier; of even greater significance is the fact that it can perform the role of 'flying crane', lifting light field artillery and vehicles into the combat zone. Some helicopters can perform all of these functions to a limited degree and the majority can perform two of the three basic roles.

The naval applications of the helicopter centre largely around anti-submarine warfare, extending the fleet's defensive zone by many miles and introducing an offensive capability. Hovering above the waves, helicopters can lower sensitive sonar devices into the water, searching for the submarine's distinctive vocabulary. Once this is located depth charges can be dropped with accuracy or a homing torpedo released to find its way to the enemy vessel. For use against surface targets naval helicopters are armed with cannon, machine guns, rockets and guided air-to-surface missiles. Other uses at sea include the transfer of stores and personnel from ship to ship or from ship to shore.

The British had had practical experience of helicopter warfare during the withdrawal from Empire and in Ulster, as well as in large scale NATO exercises; they had also studied the lessons of the Vietnam and Arab/Israeli wars and were fully conversant with its tactical and strategic applications. In the context of the Falklands the latter were particularly important, for the harsh terrain and the lack of tracks meant that only the helicopter retained complete mobility. This factor was reflected in the numbers and types of helicopter with which the Task Force was equipped.

In contrast, the Argentine high command does not appear to have digested these lessons fully, although it was familiar with the role of the helicopter in counter-insurgency operations. It certainly did not make the fullest use of its helicopter fleet, which is reported to have consisted of two Chinooks, nine Bell UH-1Ns, two Agusta A109As and three Pumas, during the Falklands Conflict.

Argentina did, however, employ helicopters during her invasion of the Falklands and South Georgia. At Grytviken Lieutenant Keith Mills and his 22 Royal Marines riddled a troop-carrying Puma, which sharply reversed course and staggered across the bay trailing smoke to crash land on the far shore, writing itself off. Mills and his men also hit and seriously damaged an Alouette before being forced to surrender.

South Georgia was to be the scene of the next helicopter actions. On 21 April an SAS detachment was lifted by a Wessex on to the Fortuna glacier. A 100 mph (160 km/h) blizzard was blowing and the machine crashed in circumstances of almost total 'white-out'. The detachment was clearly unable to execute its mission and a second Wessex was despatched to lift them out; it, too, crashed. A third helicopter eventually succeeded in evacuating the party, which later completed its task by boat.

On 25 April patrolling Lynx helicopters caught the Argentine submarine *Santa Fe* approaching Grytviken on the surface. They attacked first with depth charges and then made several passes at the conning tower, scoring numerous hits with their machine guns and missiles. Return fire from the conning tower was ineffective and the *Santa Fe* steered an erratic course into the harbour oozing a lengthening oil slick; once she had arrived alongside the jetty her crew abandoned her.

Off the Falklands the Lynxes further demonstrated their ship-killing capability on 2 May, sinking one armed patrol vessel and reducing a second to a shambles; details of the engagement are recorded in the naval section of this book.

For the naval helicopter pilots the battle had actually begun as soon as the Task Force came within range of Argentine submarines. Like the Harrier pilots, they flew continuous patrols in every conceivable kind of weather, never quite certain that they would be able to find their parent vessels again. After HMS *Sheffield* had been sunk a new and frightening task was added to their already busy schedules – that of Exocet decoy. The theory was that a helicopter should interpose itself between the missile and the target vessel; the missile's radar brain would then adopt the helicopter as its target and conform to its movements. In this way the helicopter could draw the Exocet away from the ship, climbing sharply in the last few seconds while the missile passed harmlessly beneath. According to the manual, this hair-raising manoeuvre could be completed with a reasonable degree of safety, as the Exocet would not skim above 18 feet (5.5 metres). About this there remains some debate; HRH Prince Andrew, piloting a Sea King from HMS *Invincible*, was later to comment that an Exocet had been seen to flash past at masthead height!

Perhaps the most famous helicopter of the conflict was the Sea King which landed near Punta Arenas in Chile and was partially destroyed by its crew who claimed ingenuously to have lost their way while on patrol. Those who knew the Sea

King reflected that its range was just sufficient for a direct flight from the Task Force to Tierra del Fuego, and that one of its roles was that of troop carrier. The Chilean government reacted indignantly, and London muttered its apologies. Later, reports originating in Chile claimed that an SAS team had destroyed five Super Etendards at the Argentine air base of Rio Grande, just across the border. Equally dramatic if less clandestine was the helicopters' part in the SAS attack on Pebble Island, the raiders being efficiently lifted in and out in one of the neatest operations of the conflict.

During the British landing at San Carlos helicopters moved incessantly between ships and shore, lifting heavy weapons and hundreds of tons of ammunition and stores into the beachhead every hour, so halving the time that anchored vessels would have remained at risk had they relied solely on landing craft. The only fatalities suffered arose as a result of a tragic accident in which a Sea King crashed into the sea, killing 21 of the men aboard, the majority of them belonging to the SAS; it is believed that a sea bird flew into the machine's tail rotor just as it lifted off, sending it into an uncontrollable spin.

The helicopters continued at their work throughout the battle that raged above Falkland Sound and San Carlos Water. Whenever a raid took place they kept inconspicuously low, the blue Royal Navy machines hugging the shoreline while the green of the Army Air Corps merged into the hillsides. Two light helicopters were lost to ground fire during the pursuit of the Argentine garrison from Fanning Head, and a further light helicopter was shot down by Pucaras in the battle for Goose Green.

The first week of June found most of the available helicopter lift being used to support the 3rd Commando Brigade in its trek along the northern axis from San Carlos to Douglas, Teal Inlet and Port Stanley. The 5th Infantry Brigade had also arrived at San Carlos and had been allocated the southern axis to Port Stanley via Darwin, Fitzroy and Bluff Cove, a route which would take many days to cover on foot. A handful of Scout and Gazelle light helicopters were being used by 1st/7th Gurkha Rifles, now based at Goose Green, to search for Argentine stragglers from the battle;

these were, in fact, the only helicopters then available to Brigadier Tony Wilson, the 5th Infantry Brigade's commander.

Naturally, Brigadier Wilson was anxious to learn the nature of the opposition along his axis of advance, particularly as it was flanked to the north by a range of hills on which the enemy was thought to have observation posts. Someone told him that a private telephone line ran from a house near Swan Inlet to the home of Mr Reg Binney, the farm manager at Fitzroy, and that it was probably still working. The Brigadier immediately formed his few helicopters – only two of which were armed – into an impromptu assault squadron and, with men from the 2nd Battalion, The Parachute Regiment aboard, sent them off to Swan Inlet to discover the truth.

The line was indeed still working and Binney was able to tell the paratroops that the enemy had not only withdrawn from Fitzroy but from Bluff Cove as well, leaving the bridge connecting the two settlements only slightly damaged. Wilson was advised of this totally unexpected development and promptly ordered the little squadron to press on and take possession while he mustered reinforcements.

It was at this moment that the worst effects of the loss of the *Atlantic Conveyor* became apparent, for three-quarters of the Task Force's heavy lift Chinook helicopters and one squadron of Wessex helicopters had been aboard her. One Chinook can transport 44 infantrymen, and three can transport an entire infantry company, so had they been available a whole battalion could have been lifted forward in a comparatively short time. However, for the moment the remaining Chinook was busy hauling guns and ammunition up to the 3rd Commando Brigade, who were already in contact with the numerically superior Argentine garrison of Port Stanley on the northern sector, and this job held absolute priority. Nonetheless, when it returned to the beachhead Wilson commandeered it, stuffing as many paratroops aboard as the helicopter's physical dimensions permitted, and sent it off to Fitzroy. Here the small force remained in isolation for one night while arrangements were made to move the rest of the brigade into the area as quickly as possible.

The majority of the troops travelled by sea, transferring to landing craft off Lively Island and coming in during the hours of darkness. Some, however, remained aboard the landing ships *Sir Galahad* and *Sir Tristram* and sailed right into Bluff Cove, where they suffered severely as a result of the Argentine air attack on 8 June. On this day helicopter pilots time and again ploughed through the dense smoke that enshrouded *Sir Galahad*, now an inferno of flames and exploding ammunition, winching men from the deck or from the sea and using the down-draft of their rotors to push rubber life rafts away from patches of burning oil.

Despite the heavy casualties incurred at Bluff Cove the operation as a whole was a success which secured the last potential bottleneck on the southern route to Port Stanley and brought the 5th Infantry Brigade into the line several days earlier than had been expected. It was a coup which intelligent use of the helicopter had made possible and which undoubtedly shortened the war.

The loss of the *Atlantic Conveyor* in fact reduced the Task Force's medium lift capability to one Chinook, 20 Sea Kings and 17 Wessex. The situation eased slightly with the arrival of four more Chinooks aboard the *Contender Bezant* on 10 June.

Helicopters, too, completed the logistic build-up for Major-General Moore's decisive assault on Port Stanley. Day and night they clattered over the inhospitable moorland separating San Carlos from the hills overlooking the capital, cargo nets bulging with ammunition boxes for the ever-hungry 105 mm guns, returning with wounded to the field hospitals. Only helicopters could have performed this remarkable feat of supply, for the nature of the terrain inhibited the use of conventional wheeled transport and suitable tracked carriers were in very short supply.

Had an adequate helicopter lift not been available it could have taken weeks to prepare the final attack, and during that time the troops would have had to live rough through the worst of the Falklands winter while the warships, some with unrepaired damage, rode out the gales and remained at risk from air attack. Such had evidently been General Menendez' appreciation and in the light of this he had decided to fight a defensive battle around Port Stanley, believing that the wild hinterland would keep the British at bay for a considerable period and also erode their strength. It was the helicopter which was no doubt uppermost in his thoughts when he claimed that he had been defeated by superior equipment.

It was in fact an audacious attack by a Wessex on 12 June which came close to eliminating his headquarters and staff in one blow during the daily conference at Port Stanley Town Hall. Flown by PO Ball, the Wessex launched an AS.12 missile which narrowly missed its target and blew the roof off the nearby police station. The Wessex escaped in the confusion and the enemy's anti-aircraft batteries shot down one of their few remaining helicopters.

Albeit that the Falklands Conflict was small in scale and fought in unusual circumstances, it demonstrated for the first time the employment of the helicopter in a strategic rather than a tactical role; it also demonstrated that any commander who has not digested the full implications of helicopter warfare is at a severe disadvantage.

3

The air battle – fixed wing aircraft

I. THE HARDWARE

AERMACCHI MB326GB

Designation: two-seater light attack trainer
Engines: Rolls-Royce Viper 20 turbojet with 3,410 lbs
           (1,547 kg) thrust
Speed: 539 mph (867 km/h)
Operational ceiling: 39,000 ft (11,890 m)
Range: 1,150 miles (1,850 km)
Armament: 2 × 7.7 mm machine guns in fuselage
            6 under-wing hardpoints for cannon, rocket
            pods or bombs
In service with: Comando de Aviacion Naval Argentina

AERMACCHI MB339A

Designation: two-seater light attack trainer
Engine: Rolls-Royce Viper 632-43 turbojet with 4,000 lbs
          (1,814 kg) thrust
Speed: 558 mph (898 km/h)
Operational ceiling: 48,000 ft (14,630 m)
Range: 1,039 miles (1,672 km)
Armament: 2 × 30 mm cannon
            4 under-wing hardpoints for bombs, missiles
            or rocket pods
In service with: Comando de Aviacion Naval Argentina

Together the Aermacchi MB326GB and MB339A equipped
the CANA's first attack squadron based at Port Stanley. It
was a salvo of 68 mm rockets fired at close range by an
MB339A which finally crippled HMS *Ardent*.

AVRO VULCAN

Designation: long range medium bomber
Engines: 4 Bristol Siddeley Olympus, each with a thrust of
            20,000 lbs (9,080 kg)
Speed: (maximum) 645 mph (1,038 km/h)
            (cruising) 620 mph (998 km/h) at 55,000 ft (16,764
            m)
Operational ceiling: 65,000 ft (19,800 m)
Range: 4,600 miles (7,400 km)
            in-flight refuelling capability
Armament: nuclear bombs or 21 × 1,000-lb (454 kg) high
            explosive bombs
Crew: 5
In service with: Royal Air Force

The Vulcan was developed by A. V. Roe and Company Ltd.
of Manchester in response to an Air Staff requirement of
1947, and the first prototype flew in August 1952. The aircraft
entered production in 1955 and began joining the RAF's 'V'
bomber squadrons two years later. Since 1968 the Vulcan has
served in Strike Command and is now in the process of being
replaced by the Panavia Tornado swing-wing multi-role
combat aircraft, which has a much shorter operational radius.
Those deployed for the South Atlantic crisis flew from
Ascension Island, but their remarkable 9,000-mile (14,480
km) round trip bombing runs to Port Stanley did not quite
equal a flight made by a Vulcan in 1961 between Scrampton
Lincolnshire and Sydney, Australia, a distance of 11,500
miles (18,500 km) covered in just over 20 hours with air
refuellings over Cyprus, Karachi and Singapore.

BRITISH AEROSPACE HARRIER AND SEA HARRIER

Designation: single-seater ground attack aircraft
Engine: Rolls-Royce Pegasus 103 vectored-thrust
turbofan with 21,500 lbs (9,760 kg) thrust
Speed: (at sea level) 598 mph (962 km/h)
(at 1,000 ft (304 m)) 720 mph (1,159 km/h)
(cruising) 607 mph (977 km/h) at 36,000 ft (11,100 m)
Operational ceiling: over 55,000 ft (16,760 m)
Range: (vertical take-off) 114 miles (183 km)
(STOL with wing tanks) 828 miles (1,333 km)
Armament: 2 × 30 mm cannon with an output of 22 rounds/second
2 Sidewinder heat-seeking air-to-air missiles
5 pylons (2 beneath each wing and 1 below the fuselage) used to accommodate a variety of ground attack munitions, including rocket pods, conventional 1,000-lb (454 kg) high explosive bombs or cluster bombs
In service with: Royal Air Force
Royal Navy

Stemming from the cancelled Hawker Siddeley P.1127 project, the Harrier is known universally as a 'jump-jet', the service term for this capability being V/STOL or vertical/short take-off and landing. By varying the direction of the jet thrust the pilot is able to make his Harrier climb vertically, move sideways and even backwards, as well as performing the functions of a conventional aircraft; further, the raising or lowering of a powerful air brake in the rear of the fuselage enables rapid changes to be made in the Harrier's speed. Taken together, the unique ability provided by these features is known as vectoring in forward flight, shortened to 'viffing'. Using this technique, the Harrier pilot is able not only to force a conventional jet fighter to overshoot when attacking from astern, thus rendering itself vulnerable, but can also confuse any heat-seeking missile which an attacker has launched. Because of its V/STOL capability, the

Harrier can operate without a runway and RAF Harrier squadrons in Europe have been trained to fly from small, dispersed hides which would escape a possible pre-emptive strike by the Warsaw Pact air forces.

With the phasing-out of large carriers and their ability to launch conventional jet aircraft it was inevitable that the Fleet Air Arm should turn to the Harrier. The maritime version is known as the Sea Harrier and has a redesigned nose, a higher cockpit, has received additional proofing against the effects of weather afloat, and is fitted with the most sophisticated air combat radar used by either side during the Falklands War. As fuel consumption is heavy during vertical take-off a ski-jump is fitted to the fore-end of carrier flight decks to provide additional lift following a short run up. For simplicity, the term Harrier has been used for both aircraft throughout the text.

Without the Harrier it would not have been possible for Great Britain to have sent a Task Force into the South Atlantic. In the event, it proved to be the most revolutionary and successful weapon system of the entire conflict. Previously, it had been offered to many governments, including that of Argentina, most of whom rejected the concept as being a mechanical novelty; only the United States Marine Corps and the Indian and Spanish Navies grasped its full potential. An agreement in principle to supply Harriers to China was denounced angrily by the USSR, whose own V/STOL aircraft, the YAK-36 Forger, compares unfavourably with the British machine.

DASSAULT-BREGUET MIRAGE III

Designation: single-seater interceptor/ground attack aircraft

Engine: SNECMA Atar 9C turbojet with a thrust of 9,436 lbs (4,284 kg), and 13,230 lbs (6,006 kg) with afterburner

Speed: (sea level) 863 mph (1,389 km/h)
(at 39,375 ft (12,000 m)) 1,460 mph (2,350 km/h)

Operational ceiling: 55,775 ft (17,000 m)

Operational radius: 750 miles (1,207 km) when fitted with
                      additional external fuel tanks
Armament: 2 × 30 mm cannons
           2 wing-mounted Sidewinder heat-seeking air-
           to-air missiles, or Matra/Nord air-to-air
           missiles
           under-wing pods each capable of firing 18 × 68
           mm high explosive rockets
           bombs or a guided air-to-surface missile

In service with: Fuerza Aerea Argentina

The Mirage was developed by the French manufacturers
Avions Marcel Dassault and the prototype flew as early as
1956; the aircraft went into production in 1960. Designed for
conventional air combat, it has performed extremely well in
the hands of experienced Israeli Air Force pilots, establishing
a superiority over the MiGs flown by the Arab air forces. It
has a rate of climb enabling it to reach 49,210 feet (15,000 m)
in 6.83 minutes and its large wing area (375 ft^2 or 34.8 m^2)
gives it impressive manoeuvrability at high speeds, although
this cannot be compared in any way with the agility possessed
by the British Harrier. The Mirage's operational radius
enabled it to reach the Falklands with ease from FAA
mainland air bases; however, as the aircraft's fuel consumption rises dramatically when it is flown at combat speeds the
actual time it was able to spend over the war zone was very
limited. It is understood that the FAA was troubled by a spares
problem throughout the battle and that a number of its
Mirages remained unserviceable because of this.

DASSAULT-BREGUET SUPER ETENDARD

Designation: single-seater carrier-based attack aircraft
Engine: 1 SNECMA Atar 8K-50 single shaft turbojet with
          a thrust of 11,025 lbs (5,000 kg)
Speed: (maximum) 745 mph (1,200 km/h) at sea level
Operational ceiling: 45,000 ft (13,716 m)

Range: 1,243 miles (2,000 km) without payload, decreasing
sharply according to type of external attack stores
carried

Armament: 2 × 30 mm cannons, each with 125 rounds
Magic air-to-air missiles
pylons for bombs or rocket pods
1 AM.39 Exocet air-to-surface missile

In service with: Comando de Aviacion Naval Argentina

This aircraft is an improved version of the Etendard attack
aircraft used by the French Aeronavale and began entering
service in 1978. Its significance lies in its highly efficient
Thomson-CSF radar and Singer-Kearfott inertial navigation
and weapon aiming systems, which enable it to carry, direct
and launch the AM.39 Exocet air-to-surface missile. The
Exocet is carried under the starboard wing, partly balanced
by an external fuel tank under the port wing, but the
arrangement does nothing for the aircraft's stability or
endurance. The Comando de Aviacion Naval Argentina
began the war with ten Super Etendards.

ENGLISH ELECTRIC CANBERRA

Designation: two-seater light bomber intruder

Engines: 2 Rolls-Royce Avon 109 turbojets, each with a
thrust of 7,500 lbs (3,400 kg)

Speed: (max) 580 mph (933 km/h) at 30,000 ft (9,144 m)

Operational ceiling: 48,000 ft (14,630 m)

Range: 800 miles (1,287 km)

Armament: 3 × 1,000 lb (454 kg) bombs internally, plus 2
on under-wing pylons
20 mm or 30 mm cannon mounted beneath
fuselage

In service with: Fuerza Aerea Argentina

The Canberra first entered squadron service with the RAF in

1951 and continued to serve in the bomber role until June 1972, although long range photo reconnaissance versions remained active after this date. The Fuerza Aerea Argentina ordered twelve of these aircraft in 1972, of which nine are believed to have been operational at the outbreak of the Falklands Conflict.

FMA IA-58 PUCARA

Designation: two-seater ground attack counter-insurgency aircraft
Engines: 2 × 1,022 hp (762 kW) Turboméca Astazou turboprops
Speed: (maximum) 323 mph (520 km/h) in level flight at 10,000 ft (3,048 m)
469 mph (755 km/h) when diving
Operational ceiling: 27,165 ft (8,280 m)
Operational radius: 250 miles (400 km)
Armament: 2 × 20 mm Hispano-Suiza cannon, each with 270 rounds
4 × 7.62 mm Browning machine guns, each with 900 rounds
external attack stores can be carried on 5 points and include high explosive, anti-personnel and incendiary bombs, up to 3 Bullpup air-to-surface missiles, and napalm drop tanks

In service with: Fuerza Aerea Argentina

The Pucara takes its name from the hilltop fortresses of the Incas and is manufactured by Fábrica Militar de Aviones to an FAA specification. The aircraft is highly manoeuvrable, having a stalling speed of only 78 mph (126 km/h), and requires only a very short take-off. The two-man crew sit in tandem, the co-pilot above and behind the pilot. The canopy and the cabin floor are armour-plated against small-arms fire.

The Pucara possesses impressive firepower and did achieve minor successes during the Falklands Conflict. However, it could not compete in the air battle and failed to intimidate regular troops armed with Rapier or Blowpipe missiles or who were capable of putting up a curtain of automatic fire. On the other hand, it was the only combat aircraft the FAA could deploy and maintain on the islands.

GRUMMAN S-2 TRACKER

Designation: naval anti-submarine warfare aircraft
Engines: 2 × 1,525 hp (1,138 kW) Wright Cyclone radial piston engines
Speed: (maximum) 265 mph (426 km/h) at sea level (normal patrol) 150 mph (240 km/h) at 1,500 ft (457 m)
Range: 1,300 miles (2,100 km)
Armament: homing torpedoes or rockets and bombs mounted on 6 under-wing pylons

In service with: Comando de Aviacion Naval Argentina

The Tracker was built for the United States Navy in the 1950s and is now in service with many naval air arms. The aircraft is fitted with passive acoustic search equipment, employed jointly with acoustic echo-ranging by explosive charge.

Two S-2 Trackers form part of the normal complement of the ARA *Veinticinco de Mayo* and these, together with others flying from mainland bases, may have taken part in search operations to locate the Royal Navy's hunter-killer submarines, although no contact with them has been recorded.

HANDLEY PAGE VICTOR K2

Designation: in-flight refuelling tanker
Engines: 4 Rolls-Royce Conway 201 turbofans, each with a thrust of 20,600 lbs (9,350 kg)
Speed: (maximum) 640 mph (1,030 km/h) at 40,000 ft (12,200 m)
Operational ceiling: in excess of 60,000 ft (18,300 m)

Range: 4,600 miles (7,400 km)
Armament: none
Crew: 4

In service with: Royal Air Force

The Victor first became operational in 1956 as part of the RAF's 'V' bomber force and had been designed to reach its target by flying above the level at which a potential enemy's air and ground defences could operate. However, advances in fighter-interceptor and missile design rendered this concept obsolete.

The K2 conversion to flying tanker was made by Hawker Siddeley and began entering service in 1974. Three refuelling drogues are fitted, one under each wing for fighters and one under the fuselage for bombers and transport aircraft. Two fighters can be refuelled simultaneously at the rate of 150 gallons per minute.

By the end of May Victors had flown the equivalent of ten times round the world during operations both north and south of Ascension Island.

HAWKER SIDDELEY NIMROD

Designation: anti-submarine patrol, anti-shipping strike and maritime electronic reconnaissance aircraft
Engines: 4 Rolls-Royce Spey turbofans, each with a thrust of 12,140 lbs (5,512 kg)
Speed: (maximum) 575 mph (925 km/h)
(normal patrol) 230 mph (370 km/h)
Operational ceiling: 42,000 ft (12,800 m)
Range: 5,755 miles (9,262 km) and can be extended by fitting external fuel tanks
Armament: 9 homing torpedoes plus depth charges, or a combination of mines, bombs and depth charges, all stowed in ventral compartment
air-to-surface missiles, guns or rocket pods mounted on under-wing pylons

Crew: 12

In service with: Royal Air Force

The Nimrod was developed from the de Havilland Comet jet airliner and is regarded as one of the best aircraft of its type in service today. It can drop marker and sonobuoys and is equipped with the most modern electronic sensor and tracking devices, enabling it to observe several targets simultaneously at long range in spite of the enemy's own electronic countermeasures. When patrolling at low level it is normal for two of the aircraft's engines to be closed down.

Converted for in-flight refuelling, Nimrods based on Ascension Island flew long patrols over the South Atlantic and towards the Argentine coast, protecting the Task Force's long line of communications.

The Nimrod forms the basic platform for the RAF's own AWACS, due to enter service in 1983, and much of the additional electronic equipment is housed in a redesigned nose.

LOCKHEED C-130 HERCULES

Designation: medium-range tactical transport
Engines: $4 \times 4,508$ hp (3,363 kW) Allison T56-A-15 turboprops
Speed: (maximum) 386 mph (621 km/h)
Range: 2,487 miles (4,000 km) fully loaded
Capacity: 92 infantrymen with standard equipment, or 64 paratroopers
74 stretcher cases
light armoured vehicles and field artillery up to total payload weight of 46,901 lbs (21,293 kg)
Crew: 5

In service with: Fuerza Aerea Argentina
Royal Air Force

The FAA's Hercules formed the principal link in the air bridge between the Argentine mainland and Port Stanley.

The FAA also used the aircraft in a role for which it had not been designed – that of medium bomber.

Those in service with the RAF were modified for in-flight refuelling and flew a shuttle service between the United Kingdom and Ascension Island; some flew on to the Falklands, dropping important stores and key personnel by parachute.

McDONNELL DOUGLAS A-4 SKYHAWK

Designation: single-seater attack bomber
Engine: 1 Wright J65-W-164 turbojet with 7,700 lb (3,496 kg) thrust
Speed: (maximum) 680 mph (1,094 km/h)
Operational ceiling: 49,000 ft (14,935 m)
Operational radius: 900 miles (1,148 km/h) optimum, decreasing in relation to speed and type of attack stores carried
Armament: 2 × 30 mm cannon in wing roots, each with 150 rounds
bombs, air-to-ground or air-to-air missiles on under-wing and fuselage pylons, up to 9,000 lbs (4,086 kg) in weight
In service with: Comando de Aviacion Naval Argentina
Fuerza Aerea Argentina

The Skyhawk was developed for the United States Navy by the Douglas Aircraft Company and first flew in June 1954. Since then it has seen extensive active service, flying from American aircraft carriers off Vietnam and with the Israeli Air Force. It has the reputation of being able to absorb punishment and because of its modest dimensions (wing-span 27 ft 6 in (8.38 m), length 40 ft 4 in (12.29 m) and height 15 ft (4.57 m)) was known in American service as the 'Scooter'.

On the outbreak of the conflict the Fuerza Aerea Argentina possessed 48 Skyhawks and the Comando de Aviacion Naval Argentina had a further 20, the latter flying in varying numbers from the aircraft carrier ARA *Veinticinco de Mayo*.

II. THE ACTION

The Argentine jet-fighter pilot's reaction to the news that Admiral Woodward's Task Force was steaming south to do battle with only 20 Harriers must undoubtedly have been one of astonishment, if not downright incredulity. For the Fuerza Aerea Argentina (FAA) and the Comando de Aviacion Naval Argentina (CANA) could put up between them over 200 aircraft, a majority of which out-classed the Harrier in terms of orthodox air-to-air combat.

The backbone of Argentina's air strength lay in her 43 Mirage III fighters (this figure is thought to include a number of Daggers which are Israeli-built versions of the Mirage III) and 68 Skyhawk fighter-bombers; there were also 10 Super Etendard naval attack aircraft fitted with the air-to-surface version of the Exocet missile, 8 Aermacchi MG 326GB attack trainer/interceptors, over 30 turbo-prop Pucara ground-attack aircraft, 9 Canberra jet bombers, 8 Grumman S-2 Tracker anti-submarine aircraft and a small fleet of Huanquero and Hercules transports, supported by a variety of smaller planes and helicopters.

Numbers, however, provided only one aspect of the air battle for the Falklands. The only hard runway in the islands, that at Port Stanley, was too short for the Mirages and Skyhawks to use and they had to operate from mainland air bases over 400 miles (644 km) distant. This placed the Falklands within their operational radius, but only just, and meant that they could spend minutes only over the target zone before fuel shortage compelled them to turn for home. Naval aircraft flying from the carrier *Veinticinco de Mayo* were not, initially, inhibited in this way and did fly a protective umbrella while the Argentine invasion was taking place. After the *General Belgrano* was sunk the carrier was, of course, confined to her territorial waters and could give only minimal assistance; it seems probable that for much of the time her aircraft flew from land bases.

In placing his own carrier group within easy flying range of the Falklands, yet at the outer limit of Argentine fuel endurance, Admiral Woodward effectively secured the strategic initiative in the air war. The Argentine's overall superiority remained, but it was British aircraft which were able to operate continuously over and around the islands, while the FAA's first-line jets were only able to be present for limited periods. This placed the contest on a more equal footing and reflected certain aspects of the Battle of Britain with which the FAA's operations branch must have been familiar yet apparently ignored.

In 1940 the RAF's Fighter Command had won a similar fight against odds, and a most important element in its victory was the fact that the fuel endurance of the Luftwaffe's fighter escorts did not match that of the bombers they were intended to protect. The fighters had had to return to base before the bombers had completed their mission and the latter were thus left exposed to attacks by Hurricanes and Spitfires which inflicted heavy loss. The bomber crews complained bitterly that they were being let down, yet the means did not exist for the Luftwaffe to balance the equation; at length, it simply withdrew from a battle which it knew it could not win.

Some FAA light aircraft, including a strong contingent of Pucaras, were based on the Falklands, flying from Port Stanley and grass airstrips at Goose Green, Pebble Island and elsewhere. Hercules transports continued to rumble into Port Stanley, forming an air bridge which maintained contact with the mainland after sea communications had been cut and which brought in reinforcements and supplies for the already substantial Argentine garrison.

Admiral Woodward decided that his first priority must be to knock away the Port Stanley end of the air bridge. On 1 May a single Vulcan bomber, flying from Ascension Island and refuelled three times by Victor tanker aircraft during the round trip, attacked Port Stanley airfield. The Vulcan's high altitude operational ceiling placed it beyond the sight and hearing of those on the ground. A line of explosions erupted across the airfield but only one crater appeared in the tarmac.

This was merely the start of the attack, however. Harrier after Harrier flew the length of the airfield to release a combination of delayed action high-explosive and cluster bombs; the former caused deep craters in the runway while the multiple bursts of the latter wrecked parked aircraft, damaged installations and started fires among the stockpiled stores. There was a great deal of anti-aircraft fire, but only one 20 mm round found its mark, passing harmlessly through a Harrier's tail. Simultaneously, more Harriers attacked the airstrip at Goose Green.

The Argentine response bore all the hallmarks of haste and emotion. That evening a pair of Canberras appeared above Port Stanley. Their precise mission remains unknown but what is certain is that the ground troops were not warned to expect them. Understandably jumpy after their baptism of fire, gunners manning a surface-to-air missile battery opened fire. One Canberra exploded at once; the second, seriously damaged, turned for home but found a watery grave on the way back to the mainland. It was a bad omen and one reminiscent of an earlier war in North Africa, which had begun with Italian anti-aircraft gunners shooting down their own Commander-in-Chief, Marshal Italo Balbo, over Tobruk.

As warships closed in to hammer the airfield yet again Mirage fighters were detected by the radar picket vessels. The Harriers were scrambled and the first aerial combats took place, setting a pattern that was to be maintained throughout the war. A Mirage came into the attack from astern of a pair of Harriers, releasing missiles at one, which expertly stepped aside. Inevitably, the Mirage overshot its target and immediately became vulnerable in its turn. Flight Lieutenant Bertie Penfold, piloting the second Harrier, described what happened next: 'I was able to turn up and into the enemy. I locked a Sidewinder into his jet wake and after three or four seconds the missile hit. There was an enormous explosion and I felt quite sick. Being a pilot myself it was sad to see an aircraft explode; but it's got to be done.'

The FAA lost a second Mirage in the same way and its debriefing that night must have been interesting. The first point to emerge was that trying to tackle a Harrier with a conventional jet fighter was akin to combat with ghosts; what seemed to be a solid target one second had vanished the next. The Harrier, far from being an interesting novelty, was a very canny aircraft indeed and it was flown by pilots who had been trained for a battle against odds over western Europe. In terms of air-to-air combat the FAA never found an answer to the problem and was never able to down a Harrier in a dogfight.

The second point was that the British lack of an AWACS aircraft was being countered by pushing radar picket vessels forward of the Task Force, and these were able to give sufficient warning for the Harriers to take off and intercept. This the FAA could counter in two ways. It could approach the islands at sea-level and, whenever possible, use their land mass as a shield, so reducing the warning time provided by the ships' masthead radar; and, of course, it could eliminate the pickets themselves.

Thirdly, while Port Stanley airfield had been badly knocked about, it could be rendered usable. It is extremely difficult to render, and keep, an airfield inoperable, as the air siege of Malta had proved during World War II. Craters can be filled so that soft tyre-pressure aircraft like the Hercules can use the runway, while light aircraft can land and take off on short undamaged sections. The flow of traffic using Port Stanley was reduced to a nightly trickle, but the fact that the airfield remained in use was demonstrated by the television film which regularly reached the studios in Buenos Aires. Wishing to give the impression that the runway was inoperable and so suggest that further strikes against it were needless, the Argentines constructed circles of deep mud on its undamaged areas. These were interpreted by photo reconnaissance aircraft as shell or bomb craters, but when darkness fell they were bulldozed to one side.

At the RAF and Fleet Air Arm debriefings held on Ascension and aboard *Hermes* and *Invincible* that same night there was much cause for satisfaction. The enemy had been hit hard, losing Mirages and Canberras in the air and Pucaras and other aircraft on the ground; the Harrier had proved itself, stores had been destroyed, Port Stanley airfield damaged and its air defences proved inadequate, all without loss of any kind. The events of 1 May had provided a remarkable opening to the air battle, but they were almost immediately eclipsed by the sinking of the *General Belgrano* the following day.

The junta promptly sought its revenge. On 4 May a CANA Super Etendard took off from its mainland air base and flew east with one specific task to perform – the destruction of a British warship. At the controls was Captain Augusto Cesar Vedacarratz, the Argentine Navy's senior instructor in the use of the air-launched Exocet missile. The mission was not intentionally suicidal but Vedacarratz, an incredibly brave and determined man, chose to make it so. He had already exceeded his operational radius when HMS *Sheffield*, detached from the main body of the Task Force on radar picket duty, appeared on the Super Etendard's own radar screen. He transferred the relevant data to the missile's guidance system, went through the launch drill and released the Exocet, watching it descend to skimming height and then streak towards its target. Perhaps he saw the distant flash of the explosion and watched the tall pillar of smoke rising from the horizon; no one knows for neither he nor his aircraft were ever seen again.

The shocked reaction in the United Kingdom led to demands that air bases on the Argentine mainland be bombed; whether such a course of action would have been politically wise remains beyond the scope of this study. Ostensibly, the options available for this type of operation were very limited. The Harriers could not be risked and the only obvious alternative was to use the Vulcan bombers based on Ascension Island; that would have involved a great deal of effort for fairly modest results and could not guarantee the destruction of the remaining Super Etendards, known to be flying from airfields in the far south of Argentina. There was, however, another element present.

Argentina and her neighbour Chile have a long standing territorial dispute over several islands in the Beagle Channel and had several times been to the brink of war over them. In Chile it seemed that if the Buenos Aires junta won its war over the Falklands it would immediately capitalise on its success and seize the disputed islands as well, and in preparation for this the Chilean Navy had already sailed south to its base at Punta Arenas. The British recovery of South Georgia, and the results of the fighting on 1 and 2 May, were regarded with tacit approval by the Santiago administration, and publicly applauded by Chileans everywhere. The loss of the *Sheffield*, and the manner in which she had been destroyed, caused almost as much shock in Chile as it did in the United Kingdom, for if the Royal Navy was vulnerable, so too was Chile.

Later, reports were to appear in the British press to the effect that a secret agreement had been negotiated between London and Santiago, under the terms of which a squadron of the RAF's formidable McDonnell Douglas F-4 Phantoms, widely regarded as being among the world's finest combat aircraft, had been flown to an air base in Chile, presumably with American cooperation. The mere presence of the Phantoms was not in itself a hostile act, for goodwill visits between friendly air forces are commonplace, although in this case such a visit might be regarded as unusual. The contingency governing their use against Argentine airfields can only have related to the Task Force continuing to sustain serious loss by air attack, but such a situation did not arise. If the reports were true, Admiral Woodward must have been grateful for such additional insurance against disaster; if they were not, it was still a good piece of psychological warfare which made the FAA glance over its shoulder.

On the same day the *Sheffield* was lost a Harrier was shot down by a Blowpipe missile while strafing Goose Green airstrip. Two days later two further Harriers failed to return from their mission and are believed to have collided in bad visibility. This latter incident emphasised that simply flying from carriers in these waters was extremely dangerous, for in addition to the normal hazards of heavy seas and high winds there were sleet squalls and local fog banks which could prevent an aircraft locating its parent vessel before its fuel had been expended.

These losses reduced the number of Harriers operating with the Task Force to 17 and represented an alarming rate of attrition with the principal trial of strength to come. However, the situation had been anticipated and in the United Kingdom additional Harriers had been converted, at tremendous speed, for in-flight refuelling. These now flew directly to Ascension Island, taking nine hours to cover the journey and being refuelled en route. Some were then embarked aboard the *Atlantic Conveyor* but others flew on south, again being refuelled in flight as required, to bring the Task Force's air element up to strength. It was a remarkable achievement, speaking volumes not only for the pilots' navigational skills but also for their physical endurance.

For several days the air battle continued in a fairly low key. The Harriers continued to attack ground targets and their were brief clashes with patrolling Mirages. In these the Argentine aircraft generally released their missiles at long range and then broke away, suggesting that the FAA did not, at this stage, intend to be drawn into a battle. There were minor British successes, such as the shooting down of a Puma helicopter close to Port Stanley and the capture of the spy ship *Narwal*, and the Vulcans continued their epic bombing runs from Ascension Island. It would have been strange if General Menendez had not complained that the only aircraft his men saw were British. In the end the sinking of the *Islas de Los Estados* by HMS *Alacrity* did lead to a retaliatory attack. On 12 May a formation of Skyhawks pounced on British warships patrolling off Port Stanley. HMS *Glasgow* was holed but three aircraft were downed in quick succession by missiles. It is now thought that the attack was made by three waves of Skyhawks and that the third wave broke off on seeing the carnage inflicted on the first.

On 16 May a pair of Sea Harriers caught the Argentine blockade runner *Rio Carcarania* in Port King Bay, forcing her crew to abandon her after she had been set ablaze. The same aircraft also strafed the Argentine transport ARA *Bahia Buen Suceso* at Fox Bay.

During the night of 15/16 May the SAS carried out a raid on the Pebble Island airstrip, destroying eleven aircraft on the ground, including six Pucaras. This represented a sizeable proportion of the Argentine garrison's ground attack aircraft and the loss was described in Buenos Aires as a serious blow.

A few days later a series of rumours began to filter through Chilean sources to the effect that a further SAS raid had been made on the Argentine Naval air base at Rio Grande in Tierra del Fuego, destroying five Super Etendards. The rumours were persistent and, significantly, were neither confirmed nor denied by the junta's normally strident propaganda machine, which had thus far claimed the destruction of more Harriers than the Task Force possessed and regularly reported crippling hits on HMS *Hermes*. There is strong circumstantial evidence that such a raid did take place, and the timing of the raid suggested that the expected British landing would be made very soon.

It was for this that Brigadier Lami Dozo, the Argentine air force commander, had been husbanding the FAA's strength and when it came during the night of 20/21 May he threw all his available aircraft into the battle. The course of the action has already been described and due credit given to the courage, skill and determination of the Argentine pilots, but in the opinion of senior RAF officers the FAA's direction of the battle could be faulted on a number of counts.

First, given common agreement that the strategic objective of the operation was either to halt the landing or reduce it to impotence, there was muddled thinking on how this was to be achieved. The maximum possible damage would have been inflicted had the aircraft concentrated on the assault landing ships, merchantmen, stockpiled stores and the troops consolidating their beachhead; instead, the FAA and CANA devoted most of their attention to a mutually destructive duel with the escorting warships, and the landing continued.

Secondly, the tactical handling of the battle could have been improved. Ideally, the timing of attack waves and the angles at which they approach their target should be designed to split the defenders' fire. There was little evidence of this tactic being employed, at least with any success.

Thirdly, it was apparent that Lami Dozo had left himself without an adequate operational reserve. By the evening of 21 May the FAA had incurred very serious casualties and damage and some squadrons were clearly in need of reorganisation while their surviving aircraft were repaired. Quite possibly such a heavy rate of attrition had not been anticipated, but some contingency plan should have existed whereby squadrons based elsewhere in Argentina flew promptly into the southern air bases and relieved those that were refitting. This was the crisis not only of the battle but of the war itself yet the response of the FAA staff was turgid. On

22 May, while the British consolidated their beachhead with an iron ring of air defence weapon systems, the FAA flew no combat missions at all.

Fourthly, there was a serious fault in the FAA's bombing technique, a fault which should have been spotted and eliminated during live ammunition training. Numerous hits were being obtained on British warships but few bombs were exploding; a report released in Washington suggested that if they had Great Britain might have lost the battle. Even discounting the possible intervention of the Phantom squadron this premise is faulty, for it was not the bombs themselves which were defective but simply the manner of their delivery; had that been different the number of hits scored would almost certainly have been lower.

As a matter of elementary safety bombs do not become fully armed until after they have left the aircraft. The reason for this is obvious, for an aircraft with a damaged undercarriage and an armed bomb still aboard could blow itself to pieces during a crash landing. When a bomb is dropped a small propellor is released, spinning as it passes through the air and pushing the detonator into position; after several seconds the bomb is fully armed and will explode on impact.

During World War II near-vertical dive bombing was undoubtedly the most accurate method by which a naval target could be engaged from the air. High performance modern jet aircraft, however, are unsuitable for this role; instead, they approach low and fast, releasing their bomb like a sling-shot so that it flies in a flat trajectory through the side of the target vessel. And herein lay the root of the FAA's problem for its pilots, determined to score a kill, were delaying release until the last possible moment. This did not give the bomb sufficient time to arm itself and reduced it, in simple terms, to a 1,000-lb (454 kg) cannon ball.

One answer lay in releasing the bomb a little earlier, sacrificing guaranteed accuracy for the certainty of detonation and the knowledge that even a near miss can cause extensive damage. Another technique, particularly useful when operating above enclosed water, involves the pilot pulling back on his stick just before the moment of release; for the first part of its flight the bomb climbs in sympathy with the aircraft, and then falls in a curving trajectory towards the target, having thus been given the necessary additional time in which to arm itself.

Some Argentine pilots survived long enough to assess and correct their errors, as the subsequent attacks on *Coventry*, *Sir Tristram* and *Sir Galahad* showed, but the lesson was by no means universally learnt for the attack on HMS *Plymouth*, which took place as late as 8 June, confirmed that the old mistakes were still being made.

Meanwhile, the battle of Falkland Sound raged on. On 23 May the FAA and CANA returned to attack the warships, finally turning their attention to the beachhead the following day; by then, however, it was too late to do more than inflict a little local damage. The combined naval and beachhead air defence had held, but the experience had been far from pleasant and men were starting to grumble that the Harriers were never about when they were needed. It is, of course, very difficult indeed to combine a missile-based air defence with one's own close air cover, for the obvious reason that one inhibits the other. In fact, the Harriers were fighting their own battle out at sea and it was only the enemy survivors of this that were getting through to Falkland Sound and San Carlos Water.

Throughout, Admiral Woodward's carrier group and its escort had remained within easy flying distance of the islands, being warned by the radar pickets of the enemy's approach. Additional Harriers would take off to join those on standing patrol; the FAA's line of flight was entirely predictable and it was simply a matter of getting up-sun before attacking. The same procedure would be adopted for Mirages and Skyhawks breaking away from the action over Falkland Sound. Losses inflicted were severe and the Sidewinder became a byword for efficiency; once the Harrier's missiles had been fired its 30 mm cannon took over. By the end of the battle the *Atlantic Conveyor*'s aircraft had arrived and were beginning to fly from ground pads prepared by the Royal Engineers. 'Things are looking up', commented one pilot, mulling over the general situation. 'When we arrived the odds were ten to one; now they're only four to one!'

The destruction of the *Atlantic Conveyor* on 25 May

provided a sharp reminder that four Super Etendards and a small number of air-launched Exocets were still at large. After this, the Argentine jet aircraft retired to the mainland, emerging briefly and effectively on 8 June, but otherwise making little further contribution to the conflict.

The FAA's losses had been frightful. For every two aircraft that took off for a mission over the Falklands only one returned, and sometimes the loss ratio climbed to six aircraft out of ten. These figures are based on proven kills and take no account of seriously damaged aircraft having to ditch on their way back to base; the 400 miles (644 km) of sea separating the islands must, at times, have seemed terribly wide, especially as no search and rescue organisation existed as it did for the British. No air force in history has ever suffered a comparable rate of attrition, and the FAA could not sustain it for long.

The loss of aircraft was serious enough, but it could be made good fairly quickly and there is evidence that friendly South American governments did supply Argentina with a few replacement Mirages. The loss of pilots was far more serious, for it would be many months before fully trained replacement aircrew were available in sufficient numbers to fill the gap, although the recall of reservists might offer a temporary partial solution. Worst of all, the middle rank aircrew officers, the men who made the squadrons function, had suffered proportionately serious losses and it would take far longer to replace their experience.

Back on the islands an air battle of a different sort was now taking place. When the 2nd Battalion, The Parachute Regiment assaulted Goose Green on 28 May their attack was to have received direct air support. Low cloud, however, kept the Harriers grounded for much of the time, but the FAA did manage to put up six of its slower Pucaras. These shot down a light helicopter and then bombed and strafed the paratroops as they fought their way forward. Using small arms fire and Blowpipe missiles the 'paras' downed four of the Pucaras. The cloud cleared and the Harriers came in, attacking the enemy with cannon fire, rockets and cluster bombs.

When the Argentine garrison surrendered the following morning three more unserviceable Pucaras were captured on the airstrip. In Goose Green itself a most unpleasant surprise was waiting – the discovery of hundreds of napalm drop-tanks, many filled and ready for use, some seeping napalm and all stockpiled dangerously close to the civilian settlement. Napalm is a horrifying and indiscriminate weapon. When it is dropped the fireball consumes the oxygen for some distance around while the burning liquid sticks fast to anything it touches, inflicting an agonising death or horrible injury on anyone caught by it. The FAA certainly intended to use it against British troops and in fact had done so during the battle for Goose Green. Only one aircraft seems to have been involved and that dropped its container on the fringe of the fighting without causing death or injury.

The RAF Harriers began flying from Goose Green as the major land battle began to develop around Port Stanley. The FAA's surviving Canberras also joined briefly in the land battle, but their contribution was made from high altitude and had little effect.

Apart from the events of 8 June, the FAA ended the air/sea battle on an unorthodox note. Shallow-dive bombing attacks against shipping having produced only limited success at enormous cost, it was decided to try another method. In theory, the FAA still had seven Canberra bombers, but instead of these it was Hercules transports that appeared from time to time, their crews rolling bombs through the cargo doors to predictably little purpose. One sortie, flown against the Task Force's seaborne supply line, produced results of quite the wrong kind. Flying low to improve accuracy, a Hercules managed to hit a tanker. The bomb caused some damage but failed to explode and remained lodged in such a position that it could not be disarmed without risking a major disaster. The vessel, by coincidence also called *Hercules*, was American-owned and had nothing whatever to do with the conflict. She reached a neutral port but was eventually towed out to sea and sunk.

Royal Air Force and Fleet Air Arm fixed-wing losses during the air battle amounted to 8 Harriers out of an eventual 40 employed; of these 5 were shot down by ground fire and 3 lost in accidents, one of which took place in the United Kingdom. Losses sustained by the FAA and CANA came to 31 Skyhawks, 26 Mirages, 6 Super Etendards (1 known and 5 probable), 15 Pucaras, 1 Canberra, 1 Aermacchi attack trainer, 4 Mentor trainers, 1 Hercules transport and 3 light aircraft.

Nonetheless, the Fuerza Aerea Argentina now stood even higher in public estimation than it had before the war began. It had lost its battle but the courage of its pilots had redeemed the national honour. Its commander, Brigadier Lami Dozo, emerged as a hero and withdrew from the discredited junta shortly after hostilities ended; his political inclinations have recently led to his premature retirement.

4

The land battle

I. THE HARDWARE

AML-90 LIGHT ARMOURED CAR

More specifically known by its manufacturer's code as the AML-245 Model C, this vehicle was developed for the French Army by the Panhard organisation jointly with the Direction Technique des Armaments Terrestres and is armed with a 90 mm gun which fires fin-stabilised hollow charge ammunition to a maximum range of 2,400 metres; secondary armament consists of a coaxially mounted machine gun, but four SS.11 or similar anti-tank guided weapons can also be carried. Armoured protection is limited to 15 mm.

The AML-90 is manned by a crew of three and is powered by a Panhard 89 bhp (64 kW) engine which produces a maximum roadspeed of 56 mph (90 km/h). The Argentine Army employed one squadron of these cars on the Falklands but the harsh terrain limited the use that could be made of them beyond the perimeter of the Port Stanley defences. Two examples have been brought back to the United Kingdom by the Blues and Royals.

ARMOURED RECOVERY VEHICLES

One Centurion BARV (beach armoured recovery vehicle) forms part of the normal amphibious warfare equipment of the assault ships HMS *Fearless* and *Intrepid*. The vehicle consists of a modified Centurion tank hull and chassis fitted with a tall superstructure which is formed into a bow at the front, and it can operate in eight feet (2.4 metres) of water.

The functions of the BARV are to keep beach exits clear during assault landings, recover drowned vehicles and, if necessary, push off or haul in grounded landing craft. It is manned by a Royal Marine crew of four, one of whom is a trained diver who can work in 20 feet (6 metres) of water, attaching tow lines to drowned vehicles or cutting away underwater obstructions with oxy-acetylene equipment.

The Samson light ARV is a derivative of the Scorpion family and has the same basic characteristics. It is fitted with a heavy duty winch driven by the main engine and can exert a maximum pull of 12 tons, using a 4:1 snatch-block. The vehicle is manned by a crew of three from the Royal Electrical and Mechanical Engineers and is armed with a 7.62 mm general purpose machine gun. One Samson light ARV accompanied the Blues and Royals' Scorpion and Scimitar half-squadron throughout the campaign.

FV 180 COMBAT ENGINEER TRACTOR

The Royal Engineers' Combat Engineer Tractor is built jointly by the Royal Ordnance Factories at Leeds and Nottingham and is the only purpose-built machine of its kind in service with any of the world's armies. It weighs 16 tons, has a maximum road speed of 40 mph (64 km/h) and an exceptional cross-country mobility, as well as being fully amphibious; when afloat it is propelled by two powerful rear-mounted water-jet units. It can operate as a dozer or a digger, has a rocket-fired anchor and hawser which can be used to haul itself out of boggy ground, can be fitted with a crane, an eight-ton winch, a fender for landing pontoons and a prefabricated trackway which unrolls ahead of it when crossing soft surfaces. It can also tow trailers and operate certain ancillary equipment, including the Giant Viper mine-clearing device.

LVTP-7 LANDING VEHICLE TRACKED PERSONNEL

This vehicle is manufactured by FMC Corporation of America and is widely used by the United States Marine Corps as well as the Argentine Naval Infantry Corps. The Landing Vehicle (Tracked) family was originally developed during World War II to assist US Marine landings on

Japanese held coral islands in the Pacific.

The LVTP-7 is driven by a Detroit Diesel Motor eight-cylinder turbocharged engine producing 400 bhp (298 kW) and has a road speed of 39.5 mph (64 km/h). Afloat, it is capable of 8.5 mph (14 km/h) and is driven and steered by water jets which are discharged at the rear of the vehicle. The vehicle is armed with a single 12.7 mm machine gun and is protected by 30 mm of frontal armour and 7 mm of armour elsewhere. The LVTP-7's dimensions (26 ft 1 in (7.95 m) long, 10 ft 9 in (3.28 m) high and 10 ft 9 in (3.28 m) wide) make it excessively large for its role and indeed resemble those of a main battle tank without providing anything like the protection; in general its armour is badly arranged.

The vehicle is manned by a crew of three and can carry 25 infantrymen or, alternatively, be used for ferrying ammunition and stores from ship to shore. Naturally, with so many people packed aboard, casualties tend to be heavy when an LVTP-7 is penetrated. Access is obtained by means of a ramp which also forms the rear wall of the vehicle and which can be lowered on landing.

A company of these vehicles was employed during the Argentine occupation of Port Stanley and was subsequently withdrawn to the mainland.

SCORPION LIGHT TANK and SCIMITAR LIGHT FIGHTING VEHICLE

The Scorpion and Scimitar form part of a family of vehicles developed jointly by Alvis Ltd, the Ministry of Defence and the Military Vehicles and Engineering Establishment to replace the Saladin, Saracen and Ferret. The specification was such that weight and external dimensions had to be sufficiently low for two of the new vehicles to be air-portable aboard a C-130 Hercules transport aircraft.

Scorpion and Scimitar are constructed from aluminium alloy armour and weigh respectively 17,500 lbs (7,945 kg) and 17,100 lbs (7,763 kg). They are powered by a Jaguar 4.2 litre engine which produces a maximum roadspeed of 50 mph (80 km/h). A floatation screen can be fitted to provide an amphibious capability, propulsion by tracks alone giving a water speed of 4 mph (6.4 km/h). The vehicles can climb hills with a gradient of 1:2, operate in temperatures ranging from −32 to +52 degrees Centigrade, and they have a ground pressure of 5 psi (0.35 kg/cm²), less than that of a walking man. These features made them particularly suitably for operations on the peaty heathland of the Falklands.

The Scorpion is a light tank manned by a crew of three. It is designed to perform a wide variety of battlefield and internal security roles, as well as for use with light seaborne invasion forces. It is armed with a 76 mm gun which fires five types of ammunition – HESH, high explosive (HE), smoke, canister and illuminating. The HESH (high explosive squash head) round is effective against enemy armour up to a range of 3,500 metres and can also be used for bunker busting. A coaxial 7.62 mm machine gun is also mounted. Provision is made for the stowage of 40 rounds of 76 mm and 3,000 rounds of 7.62 mm ammunition.

The Scimitar is also manned by a crew of three and performs many of the same roles as the Scorpion. It is, however, designed specifically to destroy enemy armoured personnel carriers and armoured reconnaissance vehicles. To this end it is armed with a 30 mm Rarden gun which can fire APDS or HE rounds. The gun can fire single shots in rapid succession or bursts of up to six rounds at the rate of 90 rounds per minute, the empty cases being ejected automatically from the vehicle. The APDS (armour piercing discarding sabot) round will penetrate light armoured vehicles at up to 1,000 metres range, while the HE round can be used against transport and troops under cover up to 2,000 metres distant. One hundred and sixty-five rounds are stowed for the Rarden gun, and 3,000 rounds for the coaxial 7.62 mm machine gun.

The Scorpions and Scimitars serving in the Falklands were manned by the Blues and Royals.

ANTI-TANK ROCKETS USED IN THE ASSAULT ROLE

The 66 mm light anti-tank weapon, complete with launcher, weighs only 5.22 lbs (2.37 kg). It is operated from the shoulder and the 2.2-lb (1 kg) rocket has a range of 300 metres; once it has been fired, the launcher tube, which incorporates a sighting device, can be thrown away. The 84 mm medium anti-tank weapon is also shoulder-launched and fires a fin-stabilised projectile which has an effective range in excess of 500 metres.

The Milan anti-tank guided weapon system is normally carried in two units – the prepackaged missile weighing 24 lbs (10.9 kg) and the launch unit weighing 33 lbs (15 kg). A semi-automatic guidance system is employed in which the operator keeps his sight trained on the target while infra-red sensors track the missile's exhaust, initiating the transmission of course correction signals. Milan is effective to a range of 2,000 metres.

BRITISH 105 mm LIGHT GUN

Range: 2,500 m minimum
         17,000 m with super charge
Rate of fire: 3 rounds/minute sustained
                6 rounds/minute maximum
Elevation: $-5\frac{1}{2}°$ to $+70°$
Traverse: $5\frac{1}{2}°$ left or right
            360° on circular platform
Ammunition: HE
              HESH
              white phosphorus
              base ejection smoke
              illuminating
              target marking
Crew: 6

The 105 mm light gun began replacing the Italian 105 mm

Model 56 pack howitzer in British service during the 1970s. It is easily recognisable by its bow-shaped tubular trail, its long barrel with double-baffle muzzle brake and the absence of a gun shield. It can be towed by a one-ton truck or Land Rover and can be transported as a single load by a Puma or Sea King helicopter, or may be split into two loads for transport by Wessex helicopters.

FRENCH 155 mm FIELD HOWITZER MODEL 50

Range: 18,000 m
Rate of fire: 3–4 rounds/minute
Elevation: $-4°$ to $+69°$
Traverse: 40° left and right
Ammunition: HE
Crew: 11

This weapon is identified by its multi-baffle muzzle brake, split trail and four-wheel carriage. Four were in service with the Argentine garrison of Port Stanley.

ITALIAN 105 mm MODEL 56 PACK HOWITZER

Range: 10,200 m
Rate of fire: 8 rounds/minute
Elevation: $-5°$ to $+65°$
Ammunition: HE
                      smoke
                      AP (armour piercing)
                      target indication
                      illuminating
Crew: 6

The 105 mm Model 56 pack Howitzer is manufactured by Oto Melara of La Spezia and is one of the most successful designs to have appeared since World War II. It has been adopted by numerous countries and saw active service with the British Army in Aden. It can be towed by a long wheel-base Land Rover and breaks down into 11 loads for animal transport; it is also air-portable as a single load by Wessex helicopter and two, plus towing vehicles and crews, can be ferried by a C-130 Hercules transport. The weapon can be recognised by its multi-baffle muzzle brake and gun shield.

OERLIKON TWIN 35 mm ANTI-AIRCRAFT GUN TYPE GDF-001

Tactical range: 4,000 m
Rate of fire: 550 rounds/minute per barrel, cyclic
Elevation: − 5° to + 85° at 56°/second
Traverse: 360° at 112°/second
Ammunition: fragmentation HE incendiary with/without
tracer
AP high incendiary with tracer
Crew: 3

RHEINMETALL TWIN 20 mm ANTI-AIRCRAFT GUN

Tactical range: 2,000 m
Rate of fire: 1,000 rounds/minute per barrel, cyclic
Elevation: − 5° to + 83° at 55°/second
Traverse: 360° at 100°/second
Ammunition: HE incendiary with tracer
AP incendiary with tracer
Crew: 3, including 2 ammunition numbers

In addition to their designated role these weapons were also used by Argentine troops for fire support during the land battle.

II. THE ACTION

One remarkable fact about the British Army and the Royal Marines is that over the past 200 years there have been very few periods when they have not been engaged in active operations somewhere in the world. Since World War II alone British troops have been involved in hostilities in Palestine, Korea, Malaya, Egypt, Borneo, Cyprus, Kenya, Aden and Oman. To this cumulative and inherited experience has been added the protracted campaign against terrorism in Ulster in which soldiers know that they are permanently at risk and tune their reflexes accordingly.

Simultaneously, troops have trained incessantly and in the most demanding circumstances for the possibility of all-out war with the Warsaw Pact countries. The majority of this training takes place in West Germany but the Royal Marines carry out regular exercises in northern Norway and consequently are quite familiar with the sort of climatic conditions and terrain to be found on the Falklands. All NATO armies strive to substitute quality for quantity, which is not simply a matter of providing better equipment but also of making the best use of the human resources at their disposal.

The British do this in a number of important ways. First, since their armed services are small but professional, a policy of selective recruitment is applied and if a man does not measure up physically, mentally or as an individual, he is not accepted. Generally, today's recruit is bigger and healthier than his World War II counterpart, and for this the Welfare State is to be thanked. There is, however, another side to that particular coin, for this very improvement in social conditions also means that the recruit has less natural immunity to hardship. This factor is allowed for in his training, which places great emphasis on physical fitness and which progressively shows him the limits to which the body can be pushed if required. He then accepts these standards as being the norm required for his chosen profession.

Secondly, great pains are taken to develop the qualities of

personal initiative and leadership at every level. Mere participation is no longer enough; what is required is constructive contribution. Should his immediate superior become a casualty, the junior officer, NCO or soldier is expected to take over and finish the job in hand, using his own skill and judgement. Again, as his career progresses, the officer or soldier is automatically familiarised with the workings of the system two stages above his own rank.

Thirdly, the soldier receives thorough training in the operation, care and maintenance of his weapon systems and in circumstances where expenditure of live ammunition on any large scale is inhibited by expense, electronic simulators are used to develop his skills fully. The infantryman still relies on the rifle, light machine gun, machine carbine, grenade, anti-tank rocket launcher and entrenching tool as the basic implements of his trade, but the firepower available to a World War II infantry section pales into insignificance beside that possessed by its present-day equivalent, and this is reflected in the tactics for both attack and defence.

Fourthly, because of the wars fought during the withdrawal from Empire, the British Army as a whole has had to maintain a flexible outlook. There is a stark contrast between the high technology of the Rhine Army battlegroup with its tanks, self-propelled artillery and armoured personnel carriers, the daily round of anti-terrorist activity in Ulster, and an unmechanised infantry war on the Falkland Islands, yet the same soldiers can perform in all three situations.

Finally, and by no means least, there is the soldier's personal pride in the regiment of his choice, which runs in a continuous strand throughout British military history. The soldier identifies completely with his regiment which he is quite convinced is the best in the service. Thus, the Royal Marine immediately points out that he belongs to 40, 42 or 45 Commando, the paratrooper that he is a member of a specific battalion within the Parachute Regiment. The Guardsman has an unshakeable belief that the Brigade of Guards are the best infantrymen in the world and that his own battalion has something of an edge over the others. The Gurkha feels that he has no need to prove anything to anyone. That regimental spirit is a very potent factor was demonstrated on several occasions during the land battle for the Falklands.

In a rather different category are the Army's Special Air Service Regiment and the Royal Marines' Special Boat Section, both of which have earned a reputation for successful clandestine operations in all quarters of the world. Here recruiting is even more selective and applications are only considered from trained soldiers or Marines; only a small percentage of candidates ever pass the rigorous selection process. These special forces seek men with physical stamina, strong wills, balanced personalities and the compatibility to work within small teams regardless of rank. The successful candidate becomes an expert in survival and is trained for reconnaissance, surveillance, counter-insurgency and raiding. Once engaged in operations he is rarely seen but the moral effect of his presence on the enemy is considerable, for to them he is nowhere yet everywhere and is invariably dangerous. He serves one or two tours of duty with the special forces and then returns to his parent unit.

The selection of units to form the land element of the Task Force might be taken as an unwitting compliment to the Argentine Army and Naval Infantry Corps, but was in fact dictated by the simple principle of 'horses for courses'. Since the basic nature of the operation was amphibious it was logical that it should be spearheaded by Brigadier Julian Thompson's 3rd Commando Brigade (40, 42 and 45 Royal Marine Commandos), augmented by the 2nd and 3rd Battalions of the Parachute Regiment. The choice of parachute battalions to reinforce the spearhead was influenced by the severe terrain likely to be encountered once ashore and the fact that commando and airborne units demand the same high standard of physical performance from their men. Both, too, have a long established reputation for hard, aggressive fighting. The second formation detailed for the operation was Brigadier Tony Wilson's 5th Infantry Brigade, which happened to be immediately available and which consisted of the 2nd Battalion, The Scots Guards, the 1st Battalion, The Welsh Guards and the 1st/7th Gurkha Rifles. SAS and SBS personnel were also present in substantial but unspecified numbers.

It was also obvious from the beginning that the choice of

heavy weapons to support the two brigades would be influenced by the boggy terrain. Some of the going would barely support a Land Rover, so use of main battle tanks and self-propelled guns was out of the question. However, the Scorpion/Scimitar light tank series have a ground pressure which is less than that of a man, and a half-squadron of these vehicles, crewed by the Blues and Royals, was embarked. As for artillery, the helicopter-portable 105 mm light gun had been designed specifically for this type of operation and in due course the two brigades received the fire support of 30 of these weapons, manned by 4th Field Regiment RA (12) and 29th Commando Regiment RA (18), supplemented by naval gunfire. For logistic support much reliance was placed on the helicopter as the only land vehicles capable of negotiating the terrain, other than the light tanks, were the Royal Marines' few tracked Snowcats.

The Argentine land forces were very different in style and character to the British. Argentina had not fought a foreign enemy for a century and, with the exception of counter-insurgency operations, her army lacked any form of experience in modern warfare prior to the occupation of the Falklands. Inevitably, it operated by the manuals and purchased experience at a price in casualties. The backbone of the army was its regular element, which meant its officers and NCOs, and many of these men were both brave and professional in their outlook.

Much has been made of the fact that the ranks were filled with young conscript soldiers. In fact many of their opponents were very young too, and a conscript army is not necessarily a bad army, for in Korea and Malaya British conscripts had performed every bit as well as the regulars. The Argentine system, however, suffers from a number of serious flaws, not least of which is the one-year tour of duty with the colours. When the British employed conscription a two-year tour was considered necessary, based on the principle that it takes twelve months for the civilian to start thinking like a soldier, a further six to consolidate his training, leaving six in which he is of some use to the army. In contrast, some of the Argentine conscripts serving on the Falklands had barely left the drill square.

Because the regular element of the Argentine Army is both small and privileged there is an unfortunate 'us and them' relationship between officers and NCOs on the one hand and conscript soldiers on the other. For example, whereas British officers and men share the same rations in the field, the Argentine officer's daily ration pack includes such items as a half-bottle of whisky, cigarettes, a choice of meat meals and toilet paper, while the soldier's contains only uninspired stodge, although both contain religious and political tracts. There are some doubts that officers considered their men's welfare an essential part of their duties. There was never any shortage of food within Port Stanley, yet even before the British landings the further a man was stationed from the main garrison the hungrier he went; some small outlying units lived close to the edge of starvation.

A Prussian-style discipline was enforced, yet its application was not consistent. Harsh, and sometimes foolish, punishments were awarded for comparatively minor offences, yet weapon cleaning was apparently a forgotten art; some of the small arms captured had not seen oil for months and others were actually rusty.

For the majority of men, who were used to a warmer northern climate, soldiering on the Falklands was an unpleasant experience. The weather at best was cold, there was a high wind-chill factor, there were rain and sleet squalls, snow flurries, and endless wet peat-bog. Yet the clothing provided was adequate and in the opinion of many the Argentine boot was a better product than the British boot which let in water.

In a rather different category to the army were the units of the Naval Infantry Corps, sometimes referred to as marines. These units contained a higher percentage of regulars in the ranks, regarded themselves as a *corps d'elite*, and invariably fought well. There was also a group known simply as Unit 602, the Argentine equivalent of the SAS, some of whose members had just returned from a period of instruction at the latter's barracks in Hereford.

The infantry were armed with many of the same weapons used by the British, including the 81 mm mortar. In this context it is worth mentioning that after the Argentine surrender a stock of 81 mm gas shells was discovered in Port

Stanley, filled with chloro-sulphonomine, an agent which causes asphyxiation and burns, and one can only conclude that, like the napalm containers found at Goose Green, they would not have been there had they not been intended for use. Much of the Argentine night fighting equipment, such as image intensifiers and sniperscopes, was of equal quality to, if not better than, that of the British.

For artillery support the Argentines had available 30 Italian Model 56 105 mm pack howitzers, light air-portable weapons suitable for rapid deployment, plus four 155 mm howitzers which remained near Port Stanley. These are reported to have been well handled and were supplemented on occasion by the fire of twin 35 mm and 20 mm anti-aircraft guns. The 90 mm guns of the garrison's 12 Panhard AML-90 armoured cars must also have played some part in the defensive fire plan during the last stages of the land battle.

Altogether, there were rather more than 10,000 Argentine troops, of mixed quality, on the islands. Their Commander-in-Chief was Major-General Mario Menendez, who also held the appointment of Military Governor of the Islas Malvinas. Menendez arrived on the Falklands with the reputation for being a hard man, a reputation earned during counter-insurgency operations. He was, in fact, no more experienced than any Argentine general when it came to planning a campaign against regular troops equipped with modern weapons, and he was to make a number of very serious mistakes. Before discussing these, however, it is necessary to examine the military operations with which Argentina began the conflict.

During the early hours of 2 April units of the Naval Infantry Corps began coming ashore by helicopter and rubber boat all round Port Stanley. Members of Unit 602 carried out a textbook raid on the Royal Marines' barracks at Moody Brook, tossing grenades into the rooms and then shooting in to the buildings. The barracks were empty, for the Marines had long since stood to and were concentrated at Government House where they were coming under increasingly heavy fire. An attempt to rush the building rapidly collapsed when three Argentines were shot dead in the garden; three more who managed to break into the rear were quickly captured. The fight went on.

LVTP-7s were launched from their landing vessels, swam the Narrows into Port Stanley harbour, and waddled ashore to join the assault. One of the Marines' anti-tank rockets exploded against the leading vehicle, which squealed to a standstill and started to burn; the blast effect inside the cramped interior killed everyone aboard.

The Marines' detachment commander, Major Michael Norman, told Governor Rex Hunt that his men would willingly fight on but that the LVTP-7s were quite capable of smashing their way into the building; he also suggested that the detachment should break out, taking the Governor with them, and prolong resistance in the interior. In view of the large numbers of enemy now swarming ashore, Hunt decided that either course of action would result in needless loss of life and negotiated a surrender.

The engagement had cost the Argentines a possible 15 dead, an unknown number of wounded and a wrecked LVT; none of the 25 Royal Marines were hurt.

The following day it was the turn of South Georgia. When that episode ended Lieutenant Keith Mills and his handful of Marines had killed up to 15 Argentines, downed two helicopters, and ensured that a corvette would require a long spell in a naval dockyard, all at the cost of one man slightly wounded. Taken together, the two incidents were a pointer to the fact that even the best Argentine troops had much to learn about basic aggression.

On completion of their invasion of the Falklands some units of the Naval Infantry Corps returned to the mainland, taking their LVTP-7s with them, but others remained to act as a stiffener for the Army formations which now began to arrive on the island by sea and air.

The British Task Force was already at sea and there was a reasonable certainty that it would be committed to action. Nonetheless, General Menendez had plenty of time in which to put his house in order, although the manner of his doing so was a little curious. He decided that he would fight a concentric battle of defence based on the hills around Port Stanley, and since he could not be strong everywhere, such a decision was almost inevitable. In the event, his conduct of the battle was almost entirely passive, indicating the early development of a siege mentality. There was no serious attempt, for example, to write down the British forces during their long march from San Carlos, although an energetic commander would have done his utmost to inflict the maximum possible damage. In part, Menendez seems to have let himself become unduly influenced by the difficult terrain, and he also lacked the helicopter lift necessary for major offensive operations. For this deficiency he may himself be to blame, for few generals in the history of the Argentine Army have been in the enviable position of being able to demand what they think they will require as a matter of national priority. In part, he may also have considered that his troops' morale and state of training was good for defensive tasks only. There is evidence to support both views.

His eventual dispositions on East Falkland saw the bulk of his forces concentrated in and around Port Stanley, where suitable landing beaches were heavily mined, with a detached garrison on the Darwin/Goose Green isthmus, linked by a chain of observation posts on the hills overlooking the track from Port Stanley to Darwin. There were also several small isolated outposts, such as that on Fanning Head.

Given that the force at Darwin/Goose Green would probably be eliminated quite early in the land battle, the decision to deploy troops on West Falkland at all was wasteful. Altogether, some 2,000 men, or almost 20 per cent of the total Argentine strength, was employed on garrison duty at Fox Bay and Port Howard. They would have been unable to offer effective opposition to a landing had one been made on the island, and they were quickly isolated by the Royal Navy. The garrison on Pebble Island did serve a useful purpose in that it was required to guard the airstrip from which many of the ground-attack Pucaras were intended to fly.

In his initial appreciation of the situation Menendez believed that Admiral Woodward would put his troops ashore somewhere between Bluff Cove and Port Stanley, or somewhere in Teal Inlet. These were the thoughts of a landsman, for the first alternative did not offer a suitably sheltered anchorage, while the second was confined and could only be entered through easily defended narrows; further, both lay within easy reach of counter-attack by the Port Stanley garrison and these factors rendered them quite unsuitable. Nonetheless, Menendez considered that it was in these areas that the principal dangers lay and he had extensive minefields laid, partly by air, to mask them; neither these, nor any other minefield laid by the Argentines, was marked as convention demanded, so that they presented a quite indiscriminate menace to friend and foe alike.

On 25 April South Georgia was recaptured. Some details of the action have been given elsewhere, but what finally convinced the Argentines based at Grytviken to give up was a naval bombardment finely controlled by a Royal Artillery officer who had come ashore earlier with an SAS team. No shells landed within 800 yards (730 m) of the enemy, yet they burst in such obvious patterns that the garrison began to ponder its vulnerability, surrendering without firing a shot as soon as the Royal Marines established themselves ashore. The following day saw the surrender of the Naval Infantry contingent at Leith, some miles along the coast, and that of the scrap metal merchants whose activities had been used by the junta to initiate hostilities. The operation was a demonstration of the technique of minimum force and its implication was that the Argentines could either start leaving the Falklands peacefully or stay and await the consequences.

As the Task Force entered Falklands' waters SAS and SBS teams began slipping ashore, the former to learn the enemy's dispositions, strength and morale, the latter to examine potential landing sites and beach defences. These clandestine operations reached a high point with the SAS raid on Pebble Island which resulted in the destruction of 11 enemy aircraft and important radar installations. Once again a Royal Artillery officer controlled the supporting naval gunfire with meticulous accuracy while the troops went about their work. The garrison mounted a counter-attack; all British troops are trained to spot and kill the enemy's officers quickly and the raiders now put the theory into practice. The surviving Argentines turned and fled.

The landings in San Carlos Water placed the British land forces at their moment of greatest peril, yet were accomplished without loss from enemy action. Men waded ashore wondering if the darkness would suddenly be stitched with the enemy's automatic fire, but there was only silence. They moved inland to establish a perimeter, joined by the Scorpions and Scimitars until their slit trenches were complete. Back on the tide line Royal Engineer combat tractors and earth moving equipment worked to improve the beach exits and soon men, supplies, Rapier air-defence systems, vehicles and guns were arriving in an endless stream by landing craft, motorised raft and helicopter. Delighted Falklanders gave what help they could with their farm tractors and trailers. The original beachheads were expanded, linked and consolidated. It was a model operation and by the following evening the British hold was unshakeable.

In the meantime the FAA had launched its air offensive. The troops were periodically strafed but most of the enemy's attention was absorbed by the warships. Throughout the airsea battle Blowpipe and Rapier anti-aircraft weapons took their toll of Mirages, Skyhawks and Pucaras; British Aerospace, the manufacturers of Rapier, were later startled to learn that their product had actually worked while pointing *downwards* from a hill above San Carlos Water.

The build-up continued until the 3rd Commando Brigade was ready to break out. One of its units, the 2nd Battalion, The Parachute Regiment, was to secure the flank of the advance by storming the enemy's positions at Darwin and Goose Green. The remaining four would advance on foot across country towards Port Stanley, taking Douglas and Teal on the way. Local advice to Brigadier Julian Thompson, at this phase controlling the land operation, was that it just could not be done in winter. Thompson did not agree as he knew that his Marines and paratroops were superbly fit and that they would complete the march despite the enormous weight of the equipment they were carrying. 40 and 42 Commandos were lucky in that for part of the way they received some helicopter lift, but 45 Commando and the 3rd Battalion, The Parachute Regiment made the entire 50-mile (80 km) journey on foot, crossing desolate heathland and scrambling up steep, slippery mountain slopes in rain, sleet and freezing winds. The march was one of the epics of the campaign and was ultimately as decisive as a major action.

The news that the Task Force had secured a beachhead at San Carlos probably did not concern Menendez unduly. It did not affect his concept of concentric defence, the outer ring of which formed an approximate line from Teal Inlet down through Mount Kent and Mount Challenger to Fitzroy/Bluff Cove, and he seems to have felt reasonably confident that the wild country separating the beachhead from his own troops would prevent the British from assembling and maintaining a force capable of assaulting his own positions. Captured Argentine officers later admitted that the sheer physical ability of the 3rd Commando Brigade had not been allowed for in their calculations; when the brigade began to close in on their defences it was at first thought that the Task Force possessed many times the helicopter lift it actually did. The bulk of that lift, as we have seen, was devoted to hauling guns, ammunition and heavy equipment.

The opening stages of Brigadier Thompson's move went undetected but the observation posts on the hills did spot '2 Para' marching south from the beachhead towards Darwin. At this point Menendez pulled all but a handful of his troops off Mount Kent and Mount Challenger and moved them by helicopter and farm trailer into the Goose Green perimeter; there was nothing wrong with this decision, which in other circumstances might have led to a serious British repulse, *provided* more troops were sent up to occupy the two hills, particularly the 1,500-foot (457 m) Mount Kent, which overlooked every other Argentine position all the way to Port Stanley. There was plenty of time for this to be done, but it was not.

The Goose Green garrison now numbered approximately 1,700 men, including a battalion of Naval Infantry, and was supported by a troop of 105 mm pack howitzers and four automatic anti-aircraft guns, in addition to half a dozen Pucaras which were on call. Its position could only be approached across open ground along the isthmus and was laid out in depth with interlocking arcs of fire. Mortars and artillery knew the ranges to an inch and mines had been laid.

The 2nd Battalion, The Parachute Regiment, on the other hand, mustered 600 men and had only the support of its own

81 mm mortars and two 105 mm light guns which had been lifted forward. The battalion's commander, Lieutenant-Colonel H. Jones, knew the complexity of the defences and had prepared a plan which involved the progressive elimination of each position. Prior to the reinforcement of the Argentine garrison the odds had stood at one to one; now they stood at one to three, the inverse proportion of that required for a successful assault.

Darwin, the second largest settlement on the island, was taken without undue difficulty, but as soon as the paratroops began moving against Goose Green they were pinned down by artillery, mortar and heavy machine gun fire. For once the men were grateful for the spongy quality of the peat, which absorbed the shells and so deadened their effect.

The battle continued for 15 hours. Sometimes there was a lull, followed by a period of furious fighting for about 30 minutes as a company stormed a strongpoint. Having spotted an enemy post, the paratroops fired their high velocity rifles into it until it no longer fired back; if they could get close enough they hurled grenades, and since the Argentines had a preference for six-man fire trenches the results were fearful; if they could not, they used their anti-tank rockets to blast the opposition out of the way. Within the overall direction, a soldier's battle developed, a battle in which junior officers, sergeants and corporals solved local tactical problems as they arose. The intervention of the Pucaras made little difference and saw several of them shot down.

At length the moment arrived when the battalion could go no further and was completely pinned down by a machine gun complex, coming under accurate artillery and mortar fire. Robert Fox, the BBC reporter who went through the battle with them, reflected in a subsequent radio interview that in spite of their fearsome reputation the paratroops cared deeply what happened to their comrades, and that this was one of the reasons why they were such formidable fighting troops. This was certainly true of Colonel Jones, who was also in a position to know that the crisis of the battle had been reached. He led a party which dealt with the machine guns but at the cost of his own and several other lives.

Command of the battalion was assumed by Major Christopher Keeble, who got the attacking moving again, sticking to Jones' original plan. Feigning surrender, several Argentines displayed white flags and then fired on the paratroops. After that, no surrenders were accepted unless Argentines came forward unarmed and with their hands raised. Slowly the battle began to tilt in the paratroops' favour and as the cloud cleared Harriers came in low to hammer the remaining enemy posts.

By nightfall the Argentines had been penned in a half circle around Goose Green settlement. Major Keeble knew that his battalion had taken casualties but that those of the enemy were infinitely worse. The following morning he negotiated with the senior Argentine officer, Air Commodore Wilson Drozier Podrozo, who recognised that his troops were utterly demoralised and agreed to a formal surrender ceremony. The 1,400 prisoners still outnumbered the paratroops by nearly three to one. The British had incurred the loss of 19 dead and twice as many wounded; the Argentine death toll alone amounted to 250.

Of the 2nd Battalion, The Parachute Regiment, the British Chief of Defence Staff commented that their action at Goose Green ranked among the finest achievements in the Army's long history; it certainly ranked with the same battalion's epic defence of the bridge at Arnhem under the then Lieutenant-Colonel John Frost. There would be other hard-fought actions on the Falklands, but none with the same concentrated ferocity as Goose Green, which was won by a combination of good leadership, thorough training, outstanding battlecraft, regimental pride and natural aggression.

Scarcely had the echoes of Goose Green died away when the 3rd Commando Brigade captured Douglas and Teal after minor skirmishes. During one of these a detachment of Unit 602, which had been parachuted into the area some days earlier, was cornered by a Commando reconnaissance troop in an isolated farm called Top Malo House. The Marines blasted the building with anti-tank rockets, blowing off the roof and setting it ablaze. The Argentines came out fighting and only surrendered after four of them had been killed and seven wounded; three Marines were wounded in the engagement.

Still Menendez did not plug the yawning gap left in his centre. On 2 June the Marines seized Mount Kent, the few defenders of which offered only minor resistance. From the summit the details of Port Stanley were clearly visible on a clear day. The artillery established observation posts and the guns were lifted into position.

The outermost and potentially most formidable ring of Argentine defences had now been penetrated and Menendez ordered his garrisons at Fitzroy and Bluff Cove to pull back as they were now outflanked from the north. This they did with apparent haste, for the long wooden bridge connecting the two settlements was only lightly damaged and was quickly repaired by the Royal Engineers. They would probably have made a greater contribution to the battle if they had stayed put.

General Moore had now arrived and had assumed overall command of land operations. The 5th Infantry Brigade had also arrived and details of its move into the Bluff Cove area have already been given. To reinforce this, Moore ordered the half squadron of Blues and Royals which had been moving along the northern axis with the 3rd Commando Brigade, to motor directly south and join Brigadier Wilson's command. This journey could only be undertaken cross-country and was the mechanical equivalent of the Commandos' march out of the San Carlos beachhead. The Scorpions and Scimitars coped well with the soggy heathland but had a harder time of it in the hills where the sharp scree carved chunks out of their rubber track-blocks; nonetheless, they got through in good order. Their next task was to shoot in a diversionary attack designed to convince the enemy that the 5th Infantry Brigade intended moving along the coast road to Port Stanley when actually it was marching inland into the hills.

Moore paused briefly while he completed his logistic preparations for the final battle. When it began it assumed a definite rhythm, the major objectives being assaulted at night to reduce casualties. None of it was easy. The British artillery bombardment, supplemented on occasion by naval gunfire, would be answered by the Argentine guns firing defensive patterns around their positions while the mortars of both sides joined in. Paths through the minefields had to be cleared under fire by the Royal Engineers, forced to probe laboriously by hand since the enemy's plastic mines were immune to conventional detection. Assault companies would sometimes be pinned down for hours on the slopes while red tracer cracked past from positions above and flares floated brilliantly overhead. There were times when a post could only be subdued by the use of an anti-tank rocket, and in this role the Milan missile was devastatingly effective. And, because this was essentially an infantryman's war, there were others when the defenders could only be forced out with grenades or by the use of the bayonet. By first light the Argentine survivors had usually gone and, significantly, no attempts were made to recapture the ground which had been lost.

During the day the artillery continued to fire at suitable targets, directed with great accuracy by laser rangefinders. Similar devices were used by forward air controllers to direct Harrier air strikes. Helicopters brought up thousands of shells and left with the wounded of both sides. Some of the conscript prisoners were found to have been shot in the foot or leg by their own officers simply to keep them in their trenches, a sure sign that Argentine discipline was beginning to crumble.

First to fall were Mount Harriet and the Two Sisters, taken respectively by 42 and 45 Royal Marine Commandos. The advance continued along Goat Ridge. The 3rd Battalion, The Parachute Regiment had an extremely hard fight for Mount Longdon, as did the 2nd Battalion, The Scots Guards for Tumbledown Mountain. The 2nd Battalion, The Parachute Regiment had a slightly easier time taking Wireless Ridge, being supported by a troop of the Blues and Royals.

By the morning of 14 June the only high features remaining to General Menendez were Mount William and Sapper Hill. A breakthrough seemed likely and General Moore ordered the artillery programme to be intensified. The shells could be seen exploding continuously and hurling fountains of earth skywards all along the enemy-held crests. The 1st Battalion, The Welsh Guards and the 1st/7th Gurkha Rifles were preparing to attack. Suddenly, hundreds of figures were seen leaving the Argentine positions and trudging away from the front towards Port Stanley, their growing numbers silhouetted against the previous night's light snowfall. There had been a total collapse of the Argentines' will to fight and its effects were instantly contagious and irreversible. The war was over.

There was some firing inside Port Stanley, but it was confined to conscripts taking revenge on their officers. Because of this, the strict letter of the surrender terms was not adhered to and Argentine officers were allowed to retain their side arms, purely for their own protection. The rest of the Argentines were disarmed and marched out to the airfield, there to await transport to Argentina. It was some days before their homeland would agree to have them back. General Menendez, together with several other senior officers, was later dismissed; he had made a number of serious mistakes, not least of which was to underestimate the quality of his opponents.

General Moore, on the other hand, had brought a potentially difficult campaign to a rapid and successful conclusion with very few hitches. Shortly after the Argentine surrender he commented that his principal concern had been to balance the ability of his troops to maintain their fighting efficiency in the freezing conditions prevailing on the mountains against the ideal amount of ammunition required to achieve success. The artillery had started the final battle with 400 rounds per gun; when it ended some guns were down to as few as six, in spite of the fact that the helicopters had flown all night to top up supplies. There was no shortage of ammunition, but it would have taken time to lift it forward, and during that time the troops would have had to continue living rough in the depths of the Falklands winter. As it was, his calculations proved to be remarkably exact.

5

Missile systems

AÉROSPATIALE AS.11

Designed as an air-launched version of the SS.11 anti-tank missile, the AS.11 is employed both by Britain and Argentina for use from light helicopters such as the Westland Wasp or Aérospatiale Alouette, and also finds an application in the anti-ship role.

The missile weighs 67 lbs (30 kg) and is powered by two solid-propellant rocket motors, one a boost motor burning for two seconds and the other a sustained flight motor burning for 20 seconds. It flies at 335 mph (539 km/h) and has a range of 3,000 metres. Three interchangeable hollow-charge/armour-piercing warheads are available.

The operator keeps his sight trained on the target throughout the missile's flight, steering by means of a joystick which transmits signals through trailing wires to movable baffles in the sustainer motor's exhaust.

AÉROSPATIALE AS.12

The AS.12 is the air-launched version of the SS.12 guided anti-tank missile and is designed for use from medium-sized helicopters and fixed-wing aircraft. It can be employed not only against armoured vehicles but also against ships and ground emplacements.

The missile weighs 165 lbs (75 kg) and is powered by two solid-propellant rocket motors, one a boost motor burning for 1.15 seconds and the other a sustained flight motor. It flies at 580 mph (933 km/h) and has a range of 4.97 miles (8 km). Three 63-lb (29 kg) interchangeable warheads are available, one of them being an anti-personnel fragmentation round. The AS.12, therefore, has twice the range of the AS.11 while its warhead has four times the power, being comparable in its effect to a 175 mm shell.

Two command systems are available, the simpler being identical to that employed with the AS.11. The other is known as *Telecommande Automatique*, or TCA, in which the operator keeps his sight on the target while an infra-red sensor relays the angular difference between target and missile to a small computer, which then transmits corrections along trailing wire links.

AÉROSPATIALE MM.38 AND AM.39 EXOCET

The MM.38 (MM means *Mer-Mer*, or sea-sea) Exocet is an anti-ship missile employed by both the Royal Navy and the Armada Republica Argentina and is a surface skimmer with a maximum range of 26 miles (42 km). It has a 364 lb (165 kg) blast/fragmentation warhead which is designed to explode after it has penetrated the target vessel, so causing the maximum possible damage. It is driven by two rocket motors one of which provides a boost lasting several seconds after launch, while the other provides sustained power during flight; the missile travels at 600 to 700 mph (965 to 1,126 km/h).

Once the parent ship's search radar has located its target the missile is fed electronically with details of the course it is to steer and the time at which its own Adac radar homing head is to switch on, and then launched; on becoming active the Adac set acquires the target and controls the missile during the final stages of its flight.

No MM.38s were fired from warships during the conflict, but the garrison of Port Stanley did employ some on ground mountings. The exact number launched in this way is uncertain, but one did find its target.

The AM.39 (AM means *Air-Mer*, or air-sea) version of the Exocet has been operational since 1977 and has the same basic characteristics and method of operation as the MM.38. It is, however, shorter and lighter, the boost motor being smaller because of the initial velocity provided by the launch aircraft, and this has increased its range dramatically to 47 miles (75.6 km). When the AM.39 is released it descends to skimming height under the control of an inertial navigation system.

One major problem with the AM.39 is that few aircraft are equipped with the type of search radar which enables the correct data to be fed into the missile before launch, but the Super Etendards serving with the Argentine Navy can perform this role. A second problem arises in the form of human error in that the transfer of data, especially at long range, can be inaccurate; as the missile's flight proceeds the scale of error increases proportionately until a stage is reached when the Adac homing radar head cannot acquire the intended target. A careful check on the number of AM.39s fired showed that more than half missed completely.

Devastating though the results of an Exocet hit could be, they did not necessarily mean that a ship was automatically lost. In one case the nature of the vessel's construction was a contributory factor in causing the loss, as was the type of cargo in the loss of a second. A third strike, this time with an MM.38, caused casualties and damage, but the ship remained operational.

The Exocet inflicts greatest damage when it penetrates a ship's side cleanly at an angle of 90 degrees; its efficiency decreases when the angle of strike becomes oblique. Thus, ships which turned into or away from the attack stood a better chance of surviving than those which remained on course. In so doing they also shortened their radar profile and this was, on one occasion, believed to influence the missile in its ultimate choice of target. Of three AM.39s launched on 30 May, two missed their targets and the third was destroyed in flight by HMS *Avenger*'s 4.5-inch gun. Luckily, Argentina possessed few AM.39s and was unable to replenish her stock before the conflict ended.

Details of the countermeasures taken to combat the Exocet can be found in the chapters concerning the naval and helicopter battles.

AEROSPATIALE/MBB HOT

This missile has been developed jointly by the French company Aérospatiale and the German organisation Messerschmitt-Bolkow-Blohm as a replacement for the SS.11 and AS.11. Its title is derived from its official description of *Haut-Subsonique Optiquement Teleguide*.

HOT weighs 48 lbs (22 kg) and is powered by two solid-propellant rocket motors, the Bugeat boost motor burning for 0.9 seconds and the Infra sustained flight motor for 17.4 seconds. It flies at 580 mph (933 km/h) and has a range of 4,000 metres.

The missile carries a 13.2-lb (6 kg) hollow charge warhead and employs the TCA guidance system. It can be fitted to the Aérospatiale Gazelle and the Westland/Aérospatiale Lynx helicopters.

BRITISH AEROSPACE RAPIER

The Rapier is a quick reaction surface-to-air missile which can fly at a speed in excess of Mach 2 and is operational up to 10,000 feet (3,048 m). It is guided to the target either by line-of-sight radio command signals or, in darkness or poor visibility, by a tracker radar.

The launcher also incorporates a surveillance radar, an electronic interrogator which can determine when a contact is friendly, an optical tracking system (and tracking radar if conditions are appropriate) and two power units. These are designed as a modular system in which individual components can be replaced while leaving the launcher itself *in situ*. The missile is armed with a high explosive warhead fitted with an impact fuze, and is powered by a two-stage IMI solid-propellant rocket motor. The normal detachment consists of three to five men but once loaded the system can be operated by one man at the optical tracker.

The entire Rapier system can be towed by a Land Rover or lifted into position by a helicopter, and a fully tracked self-propelled version has also been developed. Rapier has been in service with the British Army and the RAF Regiment since 1971 and is employed well forward on the tactical battlefield as well as for airfield defence. It has proved to be extremely successful and has sold well abroad.

BRITISH AEROSPACE SEA DART

The Sea Dart is a long range shipboard surface-to-air or surface-to-surface missile with a range of up to 24 miles (38.6 km). It is powered during sustained flight by a Rolls-Royce Odin ramjet, supplemented during launch by a solid-propellant rocket booster motor which jettisons after burnout.

In addition to surveillance radar, the Sea Dart system employs a Marconi tracking radar in conjunction with the missile's own semi-active homing radar. The missile is mounted on a twin handling-and-launch system designed by Vickers.

Sea Dart is in service with the Royal Navy and the Armada Republica Argentina and during the conflict enhanced the reputation it had won during trials for the destruction of high and low altitude aerial targets, including incoming missiles.

BRITISH AEROSPACE SEA SKUA

The Sea Skua is a short range surface-skimming anti-ship missile developed to arm the Royal Navy's Westland/Aérospatiale Lynx helicopters. It is powered by one solid-propellant rocket motor and has a maximum range of 8.75 miles (14 km). It carries a 77-lb (35 kg) high explosive warhead which is designed to disable rather than sink the target vessel.

The operator can select one of four heights at which he wishes the missile to skim, his choice being dictated by the sea conditions at the time of the attack. The Sea Skua is fitted with a semi-active radar seeker, but operates on a simpler principle than the Exocet, homing in on emissions reflected by the target vessel from the launch helicopter's own Seaspray tracking radar.

During the campaign the Sea Skua achieved a notable record of successes, disabling one Argentine submarine and a patrol vessel, and sinking a second patrol vessel.

BRITISH AEROSPACE SEASLUG

The Seaslug is a long range surface-to-air and surface-to-surface missile installed on the Royal Navy's 'County' class destroyers. It is powered in sustained flight by an ICI solid propellant rocket motor, assisted on launch by four solid propellant booster motors which jettison on burnout.

The control system provides automatic loading, the launcher tracking the target's movements before the missile is fired. After release the missile is guided to the target along a radar beam. Although now becoming elderly, Seaslug can still attain a 90 per cent success ratio against high and low altitude targets.

Two versions, the Mark 1 and Mark 2, are in service, the former having a range of 28 miles (45 km) and the latter 36 miles (58 km); the missile can engage targets at heights in excess of 47,200 feet (14,500 m). Seaslug is armed with a high explosive warhead fitted with contact and proximity fuzes.

BRITISH AEROSPACE SEAWOLF GWS 25

Seawolf represents the next stage beyond Seacat in close-range guided missile defence against air attack and is fitted to the Royal Navy's Type 22 destroyers. It flies supersonically and during trials intercepted targets and conventional shells moving at Mach 2; it therefore has an additional application as a defence against incoming missiles. This results not simply from Seawolf's own speed but also from the very fast reaction time provided by the system's Marconi surveillance and tracking radar, and the fact that handling is fully automatic. In flight, course corrections are transmitted from the tracking radar to the missile by means of a microwave radio command link, being implemented through the movable tail surfaces.

Seawolf is only 6 ft 7 in (2 m) long and is treated as a conventional round of ammunition. This enables vertical stowage in ready-use and deep magazines, permitting larger numbers to be carried than is possible with longer magazines that require horizontal stowage; vertical stowage also gives greater immunity from underwater explosions. The missile is armed with a high explosive warhead fitted with contact and proximity fuzes.

The Seawolf GWS 25 provided one of the great success stories of the Falklands War and has attracted considerable attention. A lighter version of the system, known as Seawolf VM 40, is also available for ships down to 900 tons displacement.

EUROMISSILE ROLAND

Roland is a close range surface-to-air missile designed for battlefield use and is manufactured by a consortium of which the principle members are Aérospatiale and Messerschmitt-Bolkow-Blohm. It has a range of 6,900 yards (6.3 km) and is guided to its target by a combination of tracker radar control and infra-red heat sensor. It is powered by a two-stage solid propellant rocket motor which produces a speed of Mach 1.6; the high explosive warhead is fitted with a proximity fuze. A number of Roland systems were used by the Argentines for the defence of Port Stanley airfield, jointly with the Short Tigercat system.

FORD AEROSPACE/RAYTHEON SIDEWINDER AIM-9L

The Sidewinder was originally developed for the US Air Force and US Navy but is now one of the world's most widely used air-to-air missiles. Its success stems jointly from its proven efficiency and the fact that it is a very simple weapon system with comparatively few moving parts or electronic components.

The missile is powered by a Rocketdyne Mark 36 solid-propellant rocket motor which gives a speed of 1,980 mph (3,186 km/h) at 40,000 feet (12,192 m). It weighs 186 lbs (84.4 kg), including a 25 lb (11.35 kg) high explosive warhead, and has a range of 11 miles (17.7 km). It uses an infra-red heat-seeking device to lock onto the heated exhaust gasses emitted by an enemy aircraft, which is rapidly overtaken and destroyed.

The Sidewinder was used by both sides over the Falklands. Those fired at the nimble British Harriers scored no kills at all; those fired by the Harriers achieved the highest ratio of successes of any missile used during the conflict.

SHORT BLOWPIPE

The Blowpipe is a shoulder-launched surface-to-air missile which was developed as a private venture by Short Brothers Ltd and is now in service with the British Army, Royal Marines and, among others, the Argentine Army. The complete system weighs 46.75 lbs (21.2 kg) and consists of a launching tube and attached aiming units, the latter incorporating a monocular sight and a thumb-operated joystick by means of which command radio signals are passed to the missile's foreplanes.

The missile is armed with a high explosive warhead fitted with a proximity fuze. It is powered by a two-stage solid propellant rocket motor, the first stage ejecting the missile from its launching tube, the second igniting after it has flown a safe distance from the operator.

Blowpipe is unique in that it can engage both attacking and retiring aircraft and has obvious secondary applications in that it can also be used against bunkers, light armoured vehicles and small vessels. In British service operators become profficient with the use of electronic training simulators. The missile achieved successes for both sides during the conflict.

SHORT SEACAT and TIGERCAT

The Seacat close range surface-to-air or surface-to-surface missile was developed by Short Brothers Ltd and is powered by a two-stage solid-propellant rocket motor. It weighs 140 lbs (63.5 kg) and carries a high explosive warhead, fitted with contact and proximity fuzes, to a maximum range of 2.95 miles (4.75 km).

It is, as its name implies, a shipboard weapon and is in service with the Royal Navy and the Armada Republica Argentina. It is normally housed in a quadruple launcher linked to a director unit from which its flight is controlled to the target either manually by means of a joystick or, more recently, under automatic radar guidance.

The Tigercat is a mobile version of the Seacat used by the RAF Regiment for airfield defence since 1970. It is also in service with the Argentine Army and Naval Infantry Corps and was used during the defence of Port Stanley airfield.

TEXAS INSTRUMENTS PAVEWAY and SHRIKE

Paveway is a free fall bomb designed to home in on laser indicator light reflected from targets. Dropped from Harriers during the last days of the conflict, Paveway eliminated designated targets with pinpoint accuracy. Shrike is an air-launched missile for use against air defence radar by homing on the emissions of the enemy's radar transmitter. Shrikes launched from a Vulcan bomber eliminated a major Argentine radar installation on 31 May.

6

Elint, Sigint and psy-war

Today, Elint and Sigint (electronic and signal intelligence) devices form an indispensible part of any major nation's armoury and without them a commander can be left groping in the fog of war. Naturally, the whole area remains shrouded in secrecy, but enough is now known for it to have become clear that in this arena Argentina fought at a serious disadvantage.

It was thought at one stage that the Soviet Union might be providing the junta with some assistance, but for political reasons neither government wished to be seen in close association with the other. If any assistance was given, it was almost certainly limited in scope and passed through the medium of a suitable third party, such as Cuba. Direct contact seems to have been confined to the Argentine purchase of coastal radar sets for the defence of the mainland.

The Russians were, of course, intensely interested in the war and fired off a volley of extremely expensive Cosmos photographic and radar-sensing satellites designed to orbit the Falklands; the former were unable to penetrate the cloud cover which blanketted the war zone for much of the time, and the latter were only of limited use since the Task Force knew the times of their passage overhead and used its own electronic countermeasures. Inevitably the Russians despatched a spy ship to shadow the Task Force, but the Royal Navy has long learned to live with such minor irritants, which can be fed with junk transmissions while local business is conducted via the traditional means of flag and signal lamp. A Tupolev Bear long range maritime reconnaissance aircraft also visited the Task Force from a base in Angola. The Russians did not pursue their enquiries beyond the limits of the total exclusion zone.

The Argentines themselves shadowed Admiral Woodward's ships with a Boeing airliner and a merchant vessel, but these were chased away as the Task Force entered the war zone. The fate of their own spy ship, the *Narwal*, has been described elsewhere. It seems unlikely that they were ever able to penetrate the British cypher system or that they were able to monitor transmissions which they were not intended to hear.

The British, on the other hand, could listen to and

understand a great deal and were able to monitor the telephone link between the islands and the mainland. The call made by General Menendez to Buenos Aires shortly before the war ended, in which he described his troops' failing morale, must have been extremely useful to General Moore when it came to planning the final battle.

Undoubtedly, the United States provided a great deal of assistance to Great Britain in this field. The American surveillance satellites were, of course, as inhibited as the Russian's by the South Atlantic weather, but the findings of Blackbird high altitude reconnaissance aircraft, flying 80,000 feet (24,400 m) above the Falklands on USAF missions, were made available to the British and enabled accurate assessments to be made of the enemy's strength and dispositions while the Task Force was still sailing south. Equally important, the Americans also made available links via their communication satellites through which the Task Force, the hunter-killer submarines and London could exchange secure information; one source suggests that the SAS and SBS reconnaissance teams were equipped with radios capable of joining this dialogue, but such an extension of the system seems quite unnecessary and hardly worth the heavy risk involved. There were many such stories involving the use of satellites and Defence Secretary John Nott was to comment that they had more in common with the film *Star Wars* than with reality. The Elint and Sigint aspects of the Falklands Conflict were like any other intelligence gathering operation in that they involved painstakingly piecing together reports from friendly sources with the results produced by monitoring the enemy's communications traffic. It was in the light of the conclusions drawn that commanders made their decisions.

There were two outstanding contributions to the Elint and Sigint war, and these were both made by individuals who were amateurs only in the sense that they had no connection whatever with any intelligence agency. The first involved a British science master and his class, who had assembled sufficient electronic equipment to carry out a thoroughly absorbing long term project – the tracking of Soviet satellites. The flurry of Cosmos activity was instantly detected, correctly placed in the context of the Falklands, and the Ministry of Defence promptly informed. The second involved an exceedingly brave Falklander named Reg Silvey, who was a radio ham. Silvey had managed to send details of the Argentine invasion to a friend in England before his set was confiscated. However, he owned a smaller set which he carried round in a shopping bag, and he used this to listen to the Argentine Army's operational frequencies, recording the traffic as he did so. He then transmitted the recording on the same frequencies, causing no little confusion as the voices and procedure were entirely authentic. Had he been caught there was a real possibility that he would have been shot.

In the psychological and propaganda war Argentina had much the best of it until the end, even though a great deal of her output was crude. In this area the targets are the minds of one's own people, of neutral states, and of one's enemy. The junta controlled the radio and television networks as well as the popular press and was thus in the happy position of being able to project whatever it liked. It had immediate access to visual material flown in from the Falklands so that the first pictures the world saw of the conflict were invariably Argentine, and these were accompanied by a suitable commentary.

The Argentine propaganda machine achieved its greatest coup after the sinking of the *General Belgrano*. The impression it gave was that a fine old ship, which included a number of admirals' sons among her crew, had been needlessly and inhumanly sent to the bottom with great loss of life; what was more, the British had broken their own rules by carrying out the sinking well beyond the limits of the total exclusion zone. The return of the cruiser's shocked but game survivors was carefully orchestrated for the media. International opinion suddenly became more sympathetic to the Argentine case, while even in Britain there was a pause for thought. The destruction of HMS *Sheffield* had less emotional impact on the world at large because the loss of life was far smaller, but it enabled the propaganda machine to take the offensive by claiming that the air-launched Exocet was a wonder weapon which Argentina possessed while the British did not. Naturally, this generated concern not only within the

Task Force but also throughout the United Kingdom.

Having made a good beginning, the propaganda machine then departed from the established ground rules of the game. In this it was doubtless doing its masters' bidding, for the junta's popularity soared with every success; therefore, the junta reasoned, its people should have a diet of success, while the enemy should be vilified. The Task Force was described as a pirate fleet, while Margaret Thatcher was portrayed as a Viking, a vampire and a Nazi stormtrooper. There were endless stories of Harriers being sent tumbling in dogfights, of ships sunk, of *Hermes* and *Invincible* being damaged again and again, of soldiers dramatically repelling raids. Even failure was exploited to the full. After South Georgia had been recaptured it was announced that Argentine special forces had retired into the island's interior, from whence they would continue to fight – and this, in one of the cruellest environments on Earth. When the British landed at San Carlos they were said to be surrounded and on the verge of a second Dunkirk. Sometimes, the propaganda machine simply placed the most favourable interpretation on the facts, but most of its output was the purest fabrication. Until the very last moments the Argentine public sincerely believed that they would win the battle.

One of the odder aspects of Argentine propaganda was the story spread among troops on the Falklands that the British would butcher their prisoners; not only that, the Gurkhas would eat them! There seems to have been a genuine horror of the Gurkhas and the junta is said to have asked the government of Nepal to have them withdrawn. It was certainly not the first time such a request had been made. After the war a series of articles entitled *Los Chicos de la Guerra* began appearing in the Argentine press; in these young conscripts described their experiences. One such contained a vivid account of an attack in which Gurkhas had advanced remorselessly, brandishing their terrible kukris while all around them their comrades were blown apart; somehow, the author had managed to survive this murderous assault. The article in question was reprinted, tongue in cheek, by a British newspaper and immediately attracted a letter from the Regimental Colonel of 1st/7th Gurkha Rifles. The battalion, he pointed out, had not taken part in an action such as the one described, and it had returned from the Falklands without sustaining casualties. It is invariably a mistake to invest one's enemy with baleful characteristics, lest the fear induced outweighs the will to resist, as in this case.

The British media and press, being entirely free of government control, were free to publish what they liked. The majority, sensibly, decided that long term interests were best served by the accurate reporting of events as they occurred, whether the news was good or bad, since truth is ultimately the best propaganda of all. There was, too, a voluntary restraint in the publication of information or conclusions which might be of use to the enemy.

There was never an organised British propaganda campaign as such. In fact the Ministry of Defence, which had ample cause to distrust certain television producers, made no provision at all for journalists of any kind to accompany the Task Force, and it took the intervention of the Prime Minister before this decision was reversed. Once the action was joined it was clear that reporters, who shared every danger ashore and afloat, identified completely with the troops, and their despatches reflected the highest credit on their profession. It was felt to be a mistake that no foreign journalists were present, but Great Britain already had the full support of her NATO allies and the Commonwealth, and had facilities been offered to all there was no knowing how great the numbers requiring passage might have been.

For the first few weeks of the conflict the only visual images available were released by courtesy of Argentine sources. It took far too long for black-and-white stills, let alone colour film, to reach London from the Task Force. It was said that the technical means to resolve this communications difficulty did exist if the will had been there to employ them. This demonstrated a certain ambivalence, for while reporters on the Falklands were forbidden to comment on the poor results obtained by the FAA's late-release bombing technique or the start of the 3rd Commando Brigade's march on Douglas and Teal, details of these very subjects were appearing in British newspapers, and these could only have come from within the Ministry of Defence.

When the Argentine propaganda machine claimed that a ship had been hit it was, of course, essential to confirm or deny the fact, since this not only added credibility to the British case, but also gave some peace of mind to the families of men serving in other ships of the Task Force. Such a policy also served to convince the world that London was a more reliable source of information than Buenos Aires.

Conversely, it is foolish to confirm more damage than the enemy suspects he has done, especially if the basic facts are still in need of clarification. Thus, it was right to confirm that the FAA had seriously damaged the *Sir Galahad* and *Sir Tristram* in Bluff Cove, since the Argentines knew this themselves; but it was totally irresponsible to allow a premature and inaccurate report to slip out suggesting that the casualties might be numbered in hundreds, as the Argentines were neither aware of this nor knew the identity of the troops involved. The actual number of casualties was well below the original estimate, but the report caused widespread worry and distress until all the details were published. This took far longer than had been anticipated, even allowing for the obvious difficulties arising in what was clearly a confused situation. There was a feeling that the Ministry of Defence might be marking time, and the question was why?

Anyone with an ear to the ground knew that 1st Battalion, The Welsh Guards had suffered severely and that two of its rifle companies had been hit hard – very hard indeed, if the original estimates were accurate. An infantry battalion cannot function as such with two of its rifle companies out of action, and it began to look as though the FAA had scored a greater success than it imagined. Further, the ceremony of Trooping the Colour, the Guards' internationally renowned ceremonial showpiece, was to be held only days after Bluff Cove. On this of all days, could Buenos Aires be allowed the propaganda coup of claiming that it had eliminated a Guards battalion? Fortunately, the situation did not arise, for the Welsh Guards' casualties were less severe than had been anticipated and, having been reinforced by two companies from 40 Royal Marine Commando, they went into action as a battalion on the approach to Sapper Hill.

In terms of positive psychological warfare activity, there

was little or no chance that the British could influence Argentine thoughts on the major issues. They could, however, try to influence the Argentine conduct of the war. The psychological pressure applied to the Armada Republica Argentina by the Royal Navy's hunter-killer submarines has already been mentioned, as have the rumours relating to the presence of an RAF Phantom squadron in Chile. It did not matter whether the squadron was real or imaginary; what mattered was that the FAA could not ignore the possibility that the rumours might have some foundation.

During World War II one of the most successful British psy-war devices had been a radio station beamed at German troops based in north-western France. Know as Soldatensender Calais, it was listened to because its news broadcasts were truthful, while those of Dr Goebbels' radio stations were not; its integrity was established by the remarkably accurate and up-to-the-minute reporting of events on the German side of the Channel, events which the Germans themselves had witnessed. Having acquired its audience, Soldatensender Calais insidiously set about undermining the confidence of the troops in their leaders and even in their own weapons. Argentina having promptly jammed the BBC's World Service transmissions on the outbreak of hostilities, it was decided to set up a duplicate of Soldatensender Calais, on Ascension Island, beamed specifically at General Menendez' garrison on the Falklands and known as Radio South Atlantic. How many men listened to or were in a position to receive these transmissions remains unknown, as is their effect, for such measures are usually long term in their influence and their success depends upon an established relationship between broadcaster and listener. If they were heeded, their message was a simple one that the garrison understood only too well: they were on their own.

A further attempt to undermine the garrison's morale was the printing of leaflets in Spanish urging soldiers to surrender in their own interests and incorporating a safe conduct pass. There is some doubt that they were ever used, for the means of distribution did not exist. The best method of delivery is by means of a shell which bursts above the enemy positions, scattering the leaflets, but this type of ammunition was not available; nor could Harriers be used as a substitute and nor was it worth risking valuable helicopters in the role.

Finally, there was the question of image. Both sides wished to demonstrate that they were acting in accordance with the established usages of war and repatriated prisoners as quickly as possible The British provided medical care for the Argentine wounded, who were then transferred from the *Uganda* to one of their own hospital ships for the voyage home. The Argentines were only required to treat one captured Harrier pilot but this they did well and there is no reason to suppose that had the number been greater their conduct would have been less than proper. Again, while they did nothing which endeared them to the Falklanders there were, thankfully, no atrocity stories to report. The British were able to make some capital from the discovery of napalm at Goose Green; yet more could have been made from the gas shells found at Port Stanley, the placing of medium artillery among the houses and the painting of red crosses on senior officers' accommodation, but by then the war was over and Great Britain's allies were requesting her to take a moderate line.

The performance of the Argentine and British psy-war/propaganda machines during the war has been compared respectively with those of the hare and the tortoise. The former was certainly the faster to react and had the field to itself for much of the time, but chose to run a crooked race; the latter was initially unimpressive, got some things right and others wrong, but stuck to the truth and in the long term became the stronger contender.

Conclusion

Writing in the *Globe and Laurel*, the Royal Marines' journal, Captain D. V. Nicholls, RM, commented that, 'The Argentine Military Junta . . . did not believe that Great Britain had the political will or the military capability to carry out an opposed amphibious landing without air superiority followed by a 70-mile advance to contact on foot across difficult terrain in mid winter against odds of two to one, 8,000 miles from the UK.'

In part, the junta was largely responsible for the predicament in which it found itself, for it does not appear to have thought through any of the conflict's strategic aspects to their logical conclusions. It must have been clear from the outset that the Argentine Navy was vulnerable to the British hunter-killer submarines, and that the FAA's bases were too far from the Falklands for it to maintain adequate air superiority over the islands. It must also have been clear that once the British established themselves ashore the quality, experience and training of their troops would be telling factors in the land battle. One aspect the junta appears to have ignored altogether was the significance of the helicopter in the planning of large scale land operations.

Yet in some ways the British were extremely fortunate. They were fortunate that their two operational carriers had not yet gone for scrap or for sale as intended, and fortunate that in the Harrier they had an aircraft which could function at sea without steam catapults or angled flight decks. Without *Hermes*, *Invincible* or the Harriers, it would have been quite impossible for them to have despatched a Task Force at all. Had the junta waited only a little while longer before launching its invasion the full impact of defence economies made over a generation would have been fearfully apparent.

The Falklands Conflict was the first occasion on which western missile systems of all types were used operationally. Their success, particularly among the surface-to-air systems, was impressive. Because of its dramatic delivery and its effect when it struck a target the AM.39 Exocet air-to-surface missile achieved a formidable reputation, yet its ratio of successes was below that of other systems.

At sea, the Royal Navy did all that was asked of it. Its surface units, already stretched painfully thin to cover their commitments and threatened with a further drastic reduction in numbers, sustained losses somewhat in excess of those anticipated. The need to re-examine certain aspects of ship construction and damage control has been mentioned. In Falkland Sound the Royal Navy demonstrated that its defences could defeat mass air attack, although it seems that its ships are inadequately armed for an engagement against low-flying targets; this, of course, can be remedied by fitting high-output automatic weapons which have amply justified their reinstatement.

In the air, the Harrier's unique performance made it the outstanding combat aircraft of the conflict. It would certainly be premature to suggest that the Harrier has revolutionised air warfare, but the implications arising from its battles over the Falklands cannot be ignored by any air force.

To the Argentine Mirage and Skyhawk pilots the fullest credit must be given for the undeniable courage and self-sacrifice displayed in pressing their attacks. On the other hand, the fact that they fought with their hearts and not with their heads resulted in their adopting a fallible bombing technique. In some measure, too, poor planning and inferior staff work detracted from the results which might have been obtained.

The helicopter served as always in countless roles, including anti-submarine patrol, ship killer, Exocet decoy, stores and personnel transporter, gunship and casualty evacuation. General Menendez had relied on the difficult Falklands terrain to inhibit the movement of British troops and artillery towards Port Stanley, but the helicopter had solved that problem, so providing the first occasion in history when its presence has decisively influenced the outcome of a campaign.

The land battle had fewer lessons to offer. Both sides employed 105 mm field artillery that was well suited to the ground, and the Scorpion family of AFVs fully lived up to expectations. The ability of the British infantry to march and fight over very difficult country in winter undoubtedly surprised their opponents. Their attacks were made with a combination of controlled firepower, sustained momentum and aggression, using every weapon at their disposal, including anti-tank rockets.

If the Falklands Conflict had one lesson which applied to sea, air and land operations alike it was that simple courage and good equipment alone are no longer enough – in the end it is professionalism which wins.

Appendix

DISPOSITIONS OF MAJOR ARGENTINE UNITS PRIOR TO THE BRITISH LANDING

EAST FALKLAND

PORT STANLEY GARRISON
3rd Infantry Regiment
4th Infantry Regiment
6th Infantry Regiment
7th Infantry Regiment
25th Infantry Regiment
5th Battalion Naval Infantry Corps
601st Anti-Aircraft Battalion
Supporting arms and FAA personnel   Total: 8,400 men

GOOSE GREEN
2nd Infantry Regiment
12th Infantry Regiment
Detachment 601st Anti-Aircraft Battalion
Supporting arms and FAA personnel   Total: 1,200 men

WEST FALKLAND

PORT HOWARD
5th Infantry Regiment
9th Engineer Company (part)   Total: 788 men

FOX BAY
8th Infantry Regiment
9th Engineer Company (part)   Total: 889 men

PEBBLE ISLAND
CANA detachment   Total: 120 men

Index

Acknowledgements

Central Office of Information 1, 2, 4, 5, 6, 7, 8, 9, 10, 11, 12, 13, 14, 15, 16, 17, 18, 19, 22, 23, 25, 26, 27, 28, 30, 31, 34, 35, 37, 39, 43, 44, 45, 46, 49, 50, 51, 52, 53, 54, 55
RN Photographers/MARS 3, 33
Westland Helicopters 20
Soldier/MARS 21, 32, 42, 47, 48
Ministry of Defence 24, 38
Chris Bacon/Press Association 29
RAC Tank Museum 36
Chris Foss 40, 41